PREPARING TO DATE YOUR SOUL MATE

WINSTON TYRONE JACKSON, SR.

Rain Publishing
KNIGHTDALE, NORTH CAROLINA

Winston T. Jackson, Sr.
Address: P.O. Box 442343, Jacksonville, FL. 32222
Email: winstontjackson@yahoo.com
Twitter: @winston_jackson
Facebook: www.facebook.com/winstontjacksonsr
Website: www.WinstonTJacksonSr.com

Edited by Rain Publishing/www.RainPublishing.com
Cover Design: Trevis C. Bailey/www.SDCreativeWorks.com

Ordering Information:
Quantity sales. Special discounts are available on quantity purchases by corporations, associations, and others. For details, contact the "Special Sales Department" at the address above.

Preparing to Date Your Soul Mate/ Winston T. Jackson, Sr. —1st ed.
ISBN 978-0-9899742-2-6
Library of Congress Control Number: 2013951966

CONTENTS

ACKNOWLEDGEMENTS

Dear Lord, I thank you for giving me a heart that matches yours concerning marriage and divorce. Thank you for giving me the inspiration and the words to write this book. I pray that it blesses many souls as much as it has blessed mine.

To my lovely wife, Cathy Michele Jackson, thank you for loving me and for being patient with me throughout this process. Thanks for your confidence and support. I love you!

To my Pastors, Michael and Connie Smith, thank you for your faithfulness to God and for staying true to His Word. It has helped me grow deeper in Him and prepared me for my purpose in this life. I love you both!

To my sister-in-law Gena Williams, thank you for the many hours of tireless support. Thanks for your encouragement, your faith in me and your belief in this project. You are truly the greatest!

To my sons, Winston II and Travis, I love you guys!

To my mother, Mamie L. Jackson, thanks for keeping me focused on the Lord. I love you!

Dedication

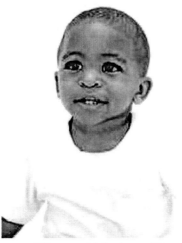

Winston T. Jackson, III

This book is dedicated to my first grandson, Winston Tyrone Jackson III. God truly blessed this entire family the day He gave life to you. I recall the day you were born, and the look in your father's eyes. It was one of total and complete love. When he passed you from his arms into mine, I thought, how precious, how sweet, how divine.

Before you were born, I prayed for you and God gave me these words for your life, "He will change a generation." That became my prayer for you since that day. Over time I began to understand what "change a generation" really meant, and now it is clear.

Your forefathers, that is, your father, grandfather and great-grandfather, did not have a clear understanding of God's purpose and design for family. We all made mistakes that caused generational dysfunction and sin within our lineage. God has placed a blessing on your life that is sure to break that trend and begin a new track and heritage for generations to come. As I write this dedication, it's been almost three years since God gave me this word. Every time I look at your father and see the man that he has become, God's word to me becomes more and more evident. Right before my very eyes I see God making your father into a true man of God, one who serves, who prays, and seeks His face. God is creating the role model that He knows you will need for your life's journey. God loves you so much that He began to first change me and now your father. The fruit of our changes is the blessed life that you will live.

So what is my prayer? What is this "changing a generation?" My prayer is based on my newly found understanding of Malachi 2:15 (GNT). Speaking to men about marriage, it says, "Didn't God make you one body and spirit with her? What was his purpose in this? It was that you should have children who are truly God's people. So make sure that none of you breaks his promise to his wife." God's desire was for children to be born of a pure and godly lineage. Your forefathers failed in that area. So my prayer is that you will come to know God at an early age. That you will chase after His love and wisdom all the days of your life. That you will maintain your virtue as God prepares a wife of the same for you. My prayer is that for the first time in this lineage, you will give birth to a child within the covenant of marriage according to God's original plan.

This book is written as a seed sown into the lives of those desiring to have a godly marriage and therefore a godly family. The harvest from this seed sown will be the day you hold your first born child in your arms and see the love of God shining through the eyes of that child as God says to you, "I love you; you have done well."   I love you,

Pop-pop

PROLOGUE

This book addresses many areas surrounding dating, courting, and searching for a mate. Most importantly, it addresses the many dynamics of a successful courtship that will prepare you for marriage. I recommend you read with paper and pen in hand to take notes. Before you begin reading the next paragraph, take a moment to pray and seek God. Ask Him to open your eyes to receive wisdom and revelation of His Word. Allow Him to reveal to you the false attractions that appear real and that you are not deceived by your own personal desires.

I must admit the title *Preparing to Date Your Soul Mate* is a bit deceiving because it implies that your desire is to meet, date and marry a person of your "soul." Truthfully, you are not looking for a person of your soul but one of your spirit, one with whom you can connect spiritually.

This is not a teaching on the soul versus the spirit; however it is important that you have an understanding of the differences between the two. Why? Because many single people are in search of their soul mate. They are looking for that one special person they can believe is "the one" for them. This can be a destructive way of thinking and can lead to major heartbreaks in your relationship.

Singles often make two mistakes as they pursue marriage: believing that there is only "one" special person out there for you and thinking that person is your "soul mate."

While reading this book, be prepared to renew your mind and the way you approach being prepared for marriage. I believe there is more than one person who could be the perfect fit as your spouse. When you allow your life to be governed by the will of God, He will send someone across your path who is a perfect match for you. Because He has given you the free will to choose, you have the option of exploring that person or moving on. The key is to be prepared when the opportunity is presented before you.

The concept of having a "soul mate" is commonly misunderstood. It is important to have a complete understanding of what your soul is and how it functions. I learned this extremely valuable lesson from my Pastor. In preparing for marriage, it is vital that your soul be made whole and complete in Christ Jesus. What do I mean by being "whole?" Wholeness is having a life where nothing is missing or broken. It is a place in your life where you are not lonely or longing for companionship. It is a state of mind where the pains of your past no longer bother you and you live a life of joy, peace and righteousness. It is the same state of mind that we see Adam in when God placed him in the Garden of Eden. Adam was not lonely, nor did he long for companionship with anyone. Adam was completely content fellowshipping with his Creator. As a single person, this is the state of mind that you want to have in order for God to bring across your path a suitable companion for your life. It was God who made the determination that it was not good for Adam to be alone. It was also God who brought woman to Adam, and she was the perfect, suitable companion for him.

Understanding the Soul

The Bible uses the term "soul" in various ways. In the case of this book, the term "soul" refers to your mind, your will and your emotions. It is what you use to think, feel, and choose. Many times the soul can be out of sync with the will of God for our lives. Therefore, we must align our soul with thinking, feeling, and choosing that agrees with the Word of God. In doing so, you think soberly and choose a mate that can connect with the Spirit of God within you. In other words man is a spirit, and he possesses a soul that lives in a body. It is your spirit man that is led, directed and guided by God. Your spirit man never loses sight of the things of God while your soul has the ability to do so. As you review the scriptures below, notice the differences between the spirit and the soul.

Soul:

Deuteronomy 6:5 NKJV "You shall love the Lord your God with all your heart, with all your soul, and with all your strength."

Psalm 23:3 NKJV "He restores my soul; He leads me in the path of righteousness for His name's sake."

Psalm 103:1 NKJV "A Psalm of David. Bless the Lord, O my soul; And all that is within me, bless His holy name!"

3 John 1:2 NKJV "Beloved, I pray that you may prosper in all things and be in health, just as your soul prospers."

Your spirit man:

Romans 8:1 NKJV "There is therefore now no condemnation to those who are in Christ Jesus, who do not walk according to the flesh, but according to the Spirit."

Galatians 5:16 NKJV "I say then, Walk in the Spirit, and you shall not fulfill the lust of the flesh."

Mark 14:38 NKJV "Watch and pray, lest you enter into temptation. The spirit is indeed willing, but the flesh is weak."

It is within the "soul" that we have our independence and free will, our freedom to choose. The terms "soul" and "flesh" are often used interchangeably. The "flesh" is not your physical skin or body tissue; it refers to your way of thinking and living. Your spirit man should be at the helm guiding you through life. Because of sin, you often lose sight of your spiritual guidance and follow your fleshly or "soul" desires.

The very first step in preparing to meet, date, and marry the person of your dreams is to master your singleness and wholeness of soul. Become whole and complete in the things of God, accepting His proposal and living life as He designed it.

Again, this is not a teaching on the soul versus the spirit; however, it is strongly recommended that you know the difference.

FOREWORD

So much of my personal life and life's work revolves around practicality and the ability to apply principles for successful daily living. If such principles cannot be achieved or lived out, they are of little use. This goes for both spiritual teachings and secular concepts.

Preparing to Date Your Soul Mate provides both godly Wisdom from the Scriptures and conventional wisdom that anyone can benefit from. Winston walks you through the entire process, beginning with the decision to totally rely on God and His ordained purpose, so you can be prepared when that special person comes into your life.

Winston has a heart for people to see God's best in their marriages. He came out of his previous marriage with compassion and empathy for couples that struggle. He knows that success begins with being properly prepared and having the right tools in your arsenal to deal with day-to-day living as a couple. His heart for marriages is revealed throughout the entire book.

While I cannot say that you will be guaranteed to meet someone and get married by reading this book, I can say that if you apply the principles outlined herein and submit to the prompting and direction of the Holy Spirit, you will be better prepared if/when that person comes along. I truly believe that God created marriage to be inherently good, but too many times couples see only glimmers of that goodness. If you have a desire to get married, or think you may in the future, do yourself (and your future spouse) a favor, and take the truths in this book to heart.

Connie M. Smith, Pastor - The Church of Jacksonville

INTRODUCTION

Psalm 127:1 Unless the LORD builds the house, its builders labor in vain. Unless the LORD watches over the city, the watchmen stand guard in vain.

Many marriages and relationships fail for one of these two reasons: right person, wrong time or right time, wrong person. I, along with many others, can make this statement, "If I had known this earlier, I could have avoided many mistakes."

It's been said that when opportunity meets preparation, there you will find success. You cannot control when an opportunity will be presented, but you can certainly be prepared when it does. Contrary to popular belief, there are plenty of good, available men and women. The problem is they cross each other's path unprepared for a relationship. Many of them either force a relationship by overlooking certain things or they simply pass each other thinking, "Could that have been the one?"

I know of a couple who knew in their hearts that they were meant to be together. They were introduced to each other under the belief that God had brought them together through a spiritual connection. Someone they mutually knew felt "led" by God to put them together and believed they were to be husband and wife. [Before I go on with the story, let me say this: it is possible for God to place on the heart or mind of someone that you should be introduced to a person as a "possible" mate. Be very careful. Consider who is speaking. Ask yourself if they have been given any spiritual authority in your life; if they have not, press the delete button and move on. Also, seek God for yourself and let Him confirm or deny this.]

So to continue the story, they married. A year later she became pregnant, and less than a year after that they separated and finally divorced. Now, in my opinion, they had the potential to become great ministering agents for God. She was indeed the right person for him as was he for her. They complemented each other so well. She was beautiful, articulate, and educated and he had a heart for God. They both wanted to serve God and use their gifts and testimonies to promote the Gospel. One big problem stood boldly before them, yet ignored. Neither prepared themselves for marriage. They failed to get premarital counseling and did not consider the inward witness that said, "Not now." Right person, wrong time. Now they have a beautiful son who loves his daddy, yet daddy lives in another state. More than anyone else, the son suffers by no fault of his own, but because mommy and daddy did not take the time to prepare for marriage.

Give God the liberty to build your relationship. Submit your way of thinking, feeling and choosing to Him and He will direct you. Unless the Lord builds your marriage, your efforts will be in vain.

The right person at the wrong time, or the right time but wrong person, will usually equal failure unless you give God the liberty to teach you His way. Why not just avoid the potential for failure by Preparing to Date Your Soul Mate, right now?

This subject of marriage and divorce is so near and dear to me because I know first-hand how important it is to life. I know how much joy and life fulfillment a godly marriage can bring. I also know through my personal experience how destructive and devastating a divorce can be. I went in to my first marriage clueless, uninformed and without counsel. After twenty-one years, divorce finally conquered that marriage leaving me, my children, and my family damaged. Thanks to God, I am married again and enjoying marriage the way God designed it. My prayer for you is to be prepared. Understand fully and completely the plan God has for marriage, then let God lead you to the perfect mate.

CHAPTER ONE

SAYING "YES" TO HIS PROPOSAL

Matthew 11:28 NLT Then Jesus said, "Come to me, all of you who are weary and carry heavy burdens, and I will give you rest. Take my yoke upon you. Let me teach you, because I am humble and gentle, and you will find rest for your souls. For my yoke fits perfectly, and the burden I give you is light."

When I proposed to my wife it was very well thought out and planned. We had already discussed marriage and we knew that eventually we would marry. I wanted to make this proposal special, memorable, and different than any other proposal I had heard of. The day started with us going to church together followed by orchestra seating for the stage play, "The Color Purple." Afterwards, I had reservations for us at Ruth's Chris Steak House. Unknown to her, I hired a photographer to hide out and take pictures of the moment. The whole restaurant staff was aware of what was going on. Our waiter was given six individually wrapped roses, each of a different color, and with a poem attached to it. The last rose was her favorite color, pink, and that one had the engagement ring attached to it. Everyone talked about how romantic and thoughtful it was. Of course she accepted my proposal, not because of the romantic gestures, but because of my proven love for God and my ability to give her all that I had promised.

The thing that made our courtship and engagement easy was that both of us were already married and fully committed to another relationship. Many years ago Jesus proposed to us individually, we accepted and fell in love with Him. Through that relationship, Jesus prepared us to meet, date and marry one another. Many years ago my wife gave her life over to Christ and allowed Him to "complete" her and make her whole. She did not have her sight on marriage at all. In fact, she had concluded that all she wanted was to live for Him. I turned my desires for a wife over to God and it was right there that God allowed us to cross each other's path. Although we were friends long before we dated, we never looked at one another with the thought "this could be the one," until God revealed it. In fact, we were not even attracted to each other that way.

This is going to be your first step in preparing for your God-ordained mate: falling in love with Jesus, courting Him and continually expressing your love for Him. While you are single, He is your spouse and the most important relationship you will ever have. It is God who will complete you, not the man or woman of your dreams.

Now back in the day when a man tried to talk to a young lady it was called "rap." These days you "holla" at a girl. If what the man was saying sounded weak, like a false advertisement for something he could not deliver, the young lady would "dis" him or dismiss him. Unfortunately, that is exactly what is happening when Jesus tries to "holla" at us, we "dis" His promises. The thing is, He can deliver and He will deliver, but only if we are willing to accept His proposal and believe Him.

In Matthew 11:28, Jesus is proposing to you. This may not seem like a "romantic" proposal, however, when you look closely at what Jesus is offering and His ability to deliver, this takes on a whole new meaning. Let's take a closer look at this proposal. He says, (paraphrased), "Marry me, and I will cause you to rest. I will ease, relieve, and even refresh your soul. Get to know me. I am gentle, meek, and humble; I have a good heart. If you get with me you'll find ease, refreshment and even recreation for your soul." When you fall in love with Him as much as He is in love with you, He will teach you how to love yourself and how to find joy within. You will get to know Him as your source for life, joy and happiness. He will become your source for health, financial stability, and true friendship.

As a woman, you will find that Jesus loves you the way you deserve to be loved. He provides for you, protects, and guides you. Your physical, spiritual and emotional well-being are a top priority for Him. When a potential mate comes along, you will be able to quickly identify if he is real or fake. You can simply look at his life and compare it to the life of your first love, Jesus. If he cannot love you, provide for you, and treat you the way Jesus does, then it is clear he is not the one. Your relationship with Jesus will prepare and teach you to love your potential mate. Jesus is the example of what a husband should be, therefore making it clear of those who are not husband material.

As a man, falling in love with Jesus gives you a role model for who you are to be for your potential wife. He will show you how to lead a righteous life before her. You will see that He places the needs of His bride before all others including Himself. Your relationship with Jesus will reveal to you the true nature and intention of a husband.

In the book of John chapter 4, beginning with verse 7, we see Jesus proposing to a Samaritan woman who had been married five times. By all indications, she felt the need for companionship, the need to love and to be loved. Perhaps she felt she needed the security of having a man in her life to provide for and protect her. She tried marriage five times and for whatever reason, it did not work out. Finally, she resorted to just living a life of fornication with a man she was not married to. Amazingly so, we see this very same situation lived out before us daily. Men and women enter into relationships or even marriage expecting to gain something from the other person. Eventually they find that the other person cannot fulfill what they need. They give up on marriage, but the desire for companionship stays with them so they repeat the same actions and eventually settle for less than they want or deserve. Many end up in an unfulfilled marriage, then seek relationships outside of the marriage to "fill the gap" of what they are missing.

Let's take a look at how this situation is played out with the Samaritan woman as Jesus proposes to her.

John 4:7-29 NKJV

A woman of Samaria came to draw water. Jesus said to her, "Give Me a drink." For His disciples had gone away into the city to buy food. Then the woman of Samaria said to Him, "How is it that You, being a Jew, ask a drink from me, a Samaritan woman?" For Jews have no dealings with Samaritans. Jesus answered and said to her, "If you knew the gift of God, and who it is who says to you, 'Give Me a drink,' you would have asked Him, and He would have given you living water." The woman said to Him, "Sir, You have nothing to draw with, and the well is deep. Where then do You get that living water? Are You greater than our father Jacob, who gave us the well, and drank from it himself, as well as his sons and his livestock?" Jesus answered and said to her, "Whoever drinks of this water will thirst again, but whoever drinks of the water that I shall give him will never thirst. But the water that I shall give him will become in him a fountain of water springing up into everlasting life." The woman said to Him, "Sir, give me this water, that I may not thirst, nor come here to draw." Jesus said to her, "Go, call your husband, and come here." The woman answered and said, "I have no husband." Jesus said to her, "You have well said, 'I have no husband,' for you have had five husbands, and the one whom you now have is not your husband; in that you spoke truly." The woman said to Him, "Sir, I perceive that You are a prophet. Our fathers worshiped on this mountain, and you Jews say that in Jerusalem is the place where one ought to worship." Jesus said to her, "Woman, believe Me, the hour is coming when you will neither on this mountain, nor in Jerusalem, worship the Father. You worship what you do not know; we know what we worship, for salvation is of the Jews. But the hour is coming, and now is, when the true worshipers will worship the Father in spirit and truth; for the Father is seeking such to worship Him. God is Spirit, and those who worship Him must worship in spirit and truth." The woman said to Him, "I know that Messiah is coming (who is called Christ). When He comes, He will tell us all things." Jesus said to her, "I who speak to you am He." And at this point His disciples came, and they marveled that He talked with a woman; yet no one said, "What do You seek?" or, "Why are You talking with her?" The woman then left her water pot, went her way into the city, and said to the men, "Come, see a Man who told me all things that I ever did. Could this be the Christ?"

This is a great story of proposal. If you look closely, you will find some very key information about this woman and about relationships in general. First, this woman was amazed by the fact that this Jewish man was even talking to her, a Samaritan. The Samaritans were considered to be inferior to Jewish people. Jewish people would not be caught talking to Samaritans, yet this particular Jewish man, Jesus, was not just talking but proposing to her. In verse 10 Jesus responds to her statement about Jewish people having no dealing with Samaritans. He says, (paraphrased), "If you knew the gift of God and who you are talking to." This is such a powerful statement to a woman who has been married many times and obviously disappointed each time. She had men before trying to "holla" at her and she fell for the game several times. They may have offered something they could not deliver, or she was expecting to get something that only Jesus could give her. But now Jesus is proposing to her with a whole new rap. He says "If you knew the gift of God..." She obviously did not know what this gift was and if she did, she did not believe in it enough to accept it. As with many of us, as a part of Jesus' proposal, He offers us this gift and we "dis" Him time after time. So what is this gift? This gift is wholeness and internal fulfillment, eternal life, peace, life, joy, love, guidance, provision and protection. These are all the things she was expecting from her previous relationships.

In verses 10 through 15, Jesus is talking about eternal life and the woman still does not get it. She thinks He is talking about physical water. Jesus finally flips the script and goes straight spiritual on this woman. He begins to get right to the root of her issue. He says to her "Go, call your husband, and come here." It was not until after He speaks about her personal business that she gets it. In verse 28, the woman was so excited about meeting this Man who could fulfill her desires, she ran off, left her water pot and told others to come meet Him.

Before you can meet, date, or marry anyone, you must accept what Jesus has to offer. Before you can offer yourself to another, you must be complete in Him meaning wholeness of mind, soul, and spirit. God wants you to depend totally on Him as your source for life. It is in your relationship with Him that you will be able to discern who is real and who is pretending. Once you have accepted Jesus' proposal and have a mature relationship with Him, you will then be in the proper position to receive the gift of a spouse from Him.

CHAPTER TWO

IN ALL YOUR GETTING, GET UNDERSTANDING

Proverbs 4:7 NKJV "Wisdom is the principal thing; Therefore get wisdom. And in all your getting, get understanding."

This proverb is often quoted by one of my spiritual leaders at the closing of his broadcast. If these words were adhered to by those desiring to be married, we would see more successful marriages. Since wisdom is so vital and important for our lives, the Bible tells us to seek it, find it, and get it! Here's the real beauty of it, getting wisdom is as simple as asking God. James 1:5 says God will give it to all men liberally and without looking at your faults. While you are seeking this wisdom, get understanding; be diligent in comprehending and applying the wisdom and understanding that you have received.

In relationships, begin with the end in mind. Your sole purpose for courting or dating should be to discover that person you would like to spend the rest of your life with, your "Soul Mate." If you are dating just for the fun of it, or it's just something to do, then you are simply practicing commitment avoidance. You are a divorced person in training. At the beginning, every relationship has the potential to take you somewhere in your life. If your desire is to one day be married, you must take dating more seriously. Just like using a road map, you have to know where you are and where you are going before you can begin to figure out how to get there. So we will start with getting an understanding of marriage and the responsibilities that come with it.

Understanding the Creation of Marriage

Why did God create marriage? What was His purpose? What was He trying to accomplish and how did He expect man to carry out His plan? What caused marriage to fail? Can we avoid failure in marriage? Knowing and understanding the answers to these questions will help prepare you for meeting your potential mate.

In the book of Genesis 1:26 NKJV, the Word says "Let Us make man in Our image, according to Our likeness." This "Us" and "Our" is referring to The Trinity; Father, Son and the Holy Spirit. Through the relationship of the Three, God made something that looked like Him and acted like Him. This is not referring to physical likeness, but a spiritual likeness, His character. Verse 27 goes on to say, "So God created man in His own image; in the image of God He created him; male and female He created them." God made man spiritually one (male and female), into something physically one (one flesh). Then He took that one physical being, made it into two physical beings, yet they remained one in spirit. Then God took the two physical beings and married them spiritually back into one flesh. In other words, in Genesis 1:27, God made a human be-

PREPARING TO DATE YOUR SOUL MATE

ing (man/Adam) in His "spiritual image and likeness." This human being was both male and female. This human being is still in the spirit form both male and female. As we look forward into chapter 2:7, we see God forming the physical or flesh of the human being He just created. It says, "And the Lord God formed man of the dust of the ground, and breathed into his nostrils the breath of life; and man became a living being."(NKJV) Let me pause and make this note. We indicated earlier that God said "Let Us" make man in "Our" image and likeness. The "Us" and "Our" was referring to the Trinity: Father, Son and Holy Ghost. As we look at this physical human being, we still see a reflection of the Trinity. We see Male, Female and the Spirit of God all present in this body of flesh. As we move down to verse 21, God took the human being, now in the flesh and caused him to go into a deep sleep. God then took the woman out of man, brought her to him and he gladly received her and recognized her importance in his life. He says, (paraphrased) "She is a part of me, because she was taken out of me." Then God says in Genesis 2:24 AMP, "Therefore a man shall leave his father and mother and shall become united and cleave to his wife, and they shall become one flesh." Now this is interesting because just a few verses ago, they were literally "one flesh" with the Spirit of God dwelling on the inside of them. Why? One reason is, man, his wife and the Spirit of God within them were to be the reflection of God upon the earth as the Trinity is in heaven. Another reason God made them, "one flesh" can be found in the writings of the prophet Malachi. Check out Malachi 2:15 (NIV), it is dealing with the issue of divorce. It says, "Has not [the LORD] made them one? In flesh and spirit they are his. And why one? Because he was seeking godly offspring. So guard yourself in your spirit, and do not break faith with the wife of your youth."

9

If you are following this closely, you will see that God made something that looks like Him, and commanded this thing to be fruitful and multiply. Then He took it, made it into two and then He brought it back together as one. For what? God's intention was for man to replicate the creation and replenish the earth by filling it with creatures that look like Him and acted like Him. He then gave this creature He called man dominion over everything in the air, under the waters and upon the earth.

What does all of this have to do with marriage? Well God expects married couples to exercise their dominion and authority upon the earth. He expects them to operate in total oneness, living and walking in His image and likeness. That means you should look like Him and act like Him. It is your God-like living that makes you fruitful. You will raise the next generation to do the same, even if they are not your biological children. Your ways of living will impact theirs, thereby creating the Godly offspring mentioned in Malachi.

Understanding the roles and responsibilities of being a husband or wife

Husband – A husband's primary role in marriage is to be a man of God. You must first learn to submit to God's authority and be governed and ruled by His Word. You must be a man who seeks godly wisdom in all that you do. If you study the life of Jesus, you will find a living breathing example of what a husband is. Ephesians 5:23-25 instructs a husband on how to love his wife by comparing the marriage relationship to the relationship of Jesus and the church. What we see in Jesus' relationship with the church is a husband that is willing to lead as He is being led by God. We see Him constantly teaching the ways of the Father and placing the needs of others before himself.

As a husband, you are charged with the responsibility of being the head of the household. Please do not misunderstand what it means to be the head of the house; you only qualify for this role when Christ is the head of you. This means you are the provider, the teacher, protector, and most of all, the spiritual leader. You are responsible for the physical and emotional well-being of the entire family. Just as Christ did, you must be willing to lay down your life for your wife, literally and figuratively. What I mean by that is, you are God's representative of His love for her. You make her "most important" in your life next to God. Your dreams, your ambitions, your life's plans are secondary to her. You place her hopes, dreams and desires ahead of your own.

Plain and simple, here is what your wife will expect from you. She wants to know that you are a "real man," willing to work and do whatever it takes to keep her and the family secure. She wants to see a spiritual leader who studies God's Word and lives God's Word. Your wife is looking for a man who prays for her and with her, as well as the children. She wants to know that she is a priority in your life, that you will choose her over all others. Your wife wants to know that she can trust you with the most precious and important things to her, that is her body, her children, and the secret places of her heart that she only shares with you and God.

The Bible is filled with instructions for a husband. While you are getting an understanding of what it means to be a husband, pick up the Word of God and search the scriptures. Being a husband is not easy, but if done with Christ as the Head of your life, you cannot lose.

Wife- As a wife, your role is very simple but not easy; why do I say that? Because it is easy to follow a man who is following Christ; however, following a fool is a completely different case.

11

That is why it is so important to take your time getting to know your potential mate before committing to him. You might say, "How will I know?" Well that is the simple part. You too must study the life of Jesus and compare His nature to the nature of your potential mate. We will speak more about that in Chapter 4, The Prep Time.

What is your role upon becoming a wife? The first step of discovering the answer to this question is, understanding who you are as a woman. God, in His infinite wisdom, created woman, and yes, you were created for man according to 1 Corinthians 11:9. You were also made a "helper," according to Genesis 2:18 NKJV. This does not mean that a woman is less than, or should be considered a second class human being. What it does mean is the role you play in the marriage relationship is to work along with your husband to accomplish God's plan for his life. Remember Genesis 1:27-28 NKJV "So God created man in His own image; in the image of God He created him; male and female He created them. Then God blessed them, and God said to them, "Be fruitful and multiply; fill the earth and subdue it; have dominion over the fish of the sea, over the birds of the air, and over every living thing that moves on the earth." At the point of creation, the Word says He made man male and female. He gave both male and female, man and woman, dominion over the fish, the birds and everything that moves upon the earth. So as a wife, you have no less dominion or authority, you simply submit your dominion and authority to that of your husband. Submitting to him as he submits to God, places you in harmony with God's intention for marriage.

Now, what will your potential husband expect or desire from you? Respect, honor and praise, that sums it up. If you want to have a husband that loves and cherishes you, learn the art of these three simple yet powerful words. Unfortunately, these words, along with the word "obey" are frowned upon by many women. Yet they are the very thing that God expects of a wife. We know that Ephesians 5:22 NKJV tells you to submit to your own husband as unto the Lord. So how do you submit to the Lord?

- In your obedience to His Word
- Respecting Him as the final authority in your life
- Honoring Him as the Head of your life
- Giving Him praise for ALL that He does in your life.

God made man and He knows better than you what it will take to please him. It is your ability to please your husband that will bring you pleasure and happiness in marriage.

Wives are to bring good into the lives of their husbands. You can make or break him. Honor, respect, and praise are basic needs of a man. Be his friend, his lover, his biggest cheerleader and even a nurturer. This does not mean treat him like a baby, but be understanding and encouraging when he is down. Also be wise enough not to allow him to stay down or wallow in self-pity.

This is not the sum of what it means to be a husband or wife, but a brief understanding. As you are Preparing to Date Your Soul Mate, seek wisdom first from God and His Word. Have casual conversations with those who have successful marriages, and with those who may have been divorced. Get a holistic view of the positives and negatives of marriages. Understand what made them work, or what contributed to the failures. Read, read, and read more to increase your understanding. Most importantly, seek God's wisdom and get understanding.

CHAPTER THREE

LIVIN' SINGLE WHILE WAITING FOR YOUR MATE

Ephesians 5:1-2 MSG "Watch what God does, and then you do it, like children who learn proper behavior from their parents. Mostly what God does is love you. Keep company with him and learn a life of love. Observe how Christ loved us. His love was not cautious but extravagant. He didn't love in order to get something from us but to give everything of himself to us. Love like that."

How you conduct yourself as a single person has a tremendous impact on the meet, date, and marry process. The harmless thing you do today can be the very thing that becomes a "deal breaker" during the engagement and cause even more trouble once you are married. It is very easy to say, "That happened long before I even met you." But the residual impact of that decision can and will creep into your marriage and cause major problems.

Your drug use, DUI, financial trouble, promiscuous lifestyle, and people you hung out with can all come back to haunt you. Remember you are building what will one day become your life's history. Today starts the experience that you will place on your relationship resume. So you will want to make it as appealing as you possibly can. Just like an actual resume, too many jobs within a short period of time will hurt your chances of landing the job you really want. Different from the job resume, long gaps between relationships may speak volumes to your own security and self-sufficiency. Having no experience at all can be a great advantage in the case of relationships. It means you can fall completely in love with Jesus and allow Him to show you how to love and to be loved. It also means that when He introduces the perfect mate to you, that person does not have your past to compete with or be concerned with.

As a single person desiring a mate, you will want the absolute BEST that God has for you. So guess what? Your potential mate has the same thought in mind; therefore, you must become the BEST that God has to offer to another. Since you cannot change your past, you must begin now to affect your today and tomorrow by living your single life according to God's Word.

Living Single

Your singleness is a very precious time of life. It is a time of transition. You are moving from being a single, whole and complete person in God, to being joined to a man or woman that is presented to you directly from God. This time should not be lived out with a total focus on getting married, although that is very important. Your single life is a time to explore God's Word. Explore who you are and why you are here. It is a time to discover the purpose and meaning of life both generally and specifically for you. Life is not about vain pursuits of happiness such as money, education, possessions or even status. Some people dream of receiving degrees or owning a business or obtaining a certain position. In some cases they achieve their goals only to find life has passed them by. It is perfectly okay to pursue these things, achieve and celebrate the successes. You must keep this in mind: accomplishments can bring you temporary happiness, not a life filled with joy. This type of joy can only be obtained in your pursuit of wholeness of soul, and that can only be found in a relationship with Jesus Christ. It is in your time of singleness that you establish this life-joy and it will prepare you for that special someone that God will certainly present to you.

Your day-to-day living should be in somewhat of a "pre" preparation time for marriage. Although your focus is not on marriage during this time, you must consider that every decision you make has the potential to impact your future as a husband or wife. Living as a good Christian with strong spiritual and moral character should be your goal. You should begin shaping and developing your character by surrounding yourself with people who are in pursuit of the same goals. Feed your mind and soul with spiritual things; avoid saturating your mind with worldly entertainment and activities. What you allow into your mind, body and soul will eventually dictate your way of thinking. The way you think will determine the actions you take and the actions you take will determine the type of life you will live. Better stated, the type of person you are will be the type of person you will attract. Become a person of godly character and that is exactly what you will attract. People who enjoy living a sinful life will find it uncomfortable to approach you. If they do, they have one purpose in mind, and that is to destroy you.

As you live the single life, embrace and enjoy these times. Live today by doing things you have promised yourself you would do. Travel, write a book, learn to play an instrument, and learn a new language. Spend time discovering you, your

17

heritage, and your way of life. Live with little emphasis on getting married, yet not forgetting that one day you could be.

Your singleness is a great time to establish the most important relationship you will ever have, that is with God the Father. He desires to be your friend. Abraham, because of his faithfulness and righteousness, was called God's friend (James 2:23). Moses, who God called friend, spoke with Him face to face (Exodus 33:11). God wants the same relationship with you. He wants to fellowship with you daily. So in your singleness, seek a friendship with God. Let Him show you what a true friend is; then surround yourself with earthly friends who reflect His nature.

Friends

Living single does not mean you become a hermit, where you withdraw yourself from society and live a life of religious seclusion. Get to know people, socialize. Get to know the right people, people who are like-minded and have similar desires as you. The people you socialize with will have a greater influence in your life than you might think.

As you enjoy life in preparation for a mate, take a close look at those you surround yourself with. Look at each individual person and take an assessment of where they are in life, where they want to be in life and their ability to get there. Ask yourself "Do they have the potential to lift me up or pull me down? Are they daydreamers full of plans but no action? Or, are they headed in the direction of living a godly life as I am?" It has been said that you are the sum total of your closest friends. So if your friends are a party crew that are constantly on the go, drinking, smoking or just hanging out, then that is who you are. But if your closest friends are having good clean wholesome fun while pursuing a better life, then so will you. This may call for you to change your destiny by changing your friends.

You may be familiar with 2 Corinthians 6:14 NJKV as it says, "Do not be unequally yoked together with unbelievers. For what fellowship has righteousness with lawlessness? And what communion has light with darkness?" In other words, do not link or be joined with those who are non-believers; those who reject God. Good and evil cannot share the same goals and passions. Since every relationship has the ability to take you somewhere, it is vitally important to not link yourself with those who are going nowhere.

Sexual Purity

The Bible warns us time after time about maintaining a sexually pure lifestyle as both married and unmarried. Many people ignore these warnings and decide to take a chance. They deceive themselves into thinking that they can handle it. This is a very sensitive area for many people simply because they are blinded to the impact sexual impurity will have on their single lives. As a single person desiring to be married, the most valuable gift you can give to your husband or wife is your sexual purity. Knowing that your husband or wife is the first and only one to have touched or seen your intimate areas brings trust, confidence and love. If it is too late to offer your future spouse your virginity, it is not too late to offer your purity. That is, begin now to purify yourself. Ask God for His forgiveness. Forgive yourself and start living a sexually pure life now.

19

When you have been with others sexually prior to your marriage, you bring the emotions and experiences of sex with those persons into the bed with your spouse. You open the door to comparisons, and imaginations of who, what, when, where and how. The question of honesty is raised and is often questioned throughout the relationship. These are doors that can remain closed and issues avoided in the future by simply maintaining your virtue as a man or a woman. However, if you have already crossed that line, it is not too late to turn yourself over to your first Love (Jesus) and allow Him to purify you. We see this in the Bible in John 8 where a woman was caught in the very act of sexual sin. Yet Jesus forgave her and cleansed her of the sin.

While I am on this subject, let me say this to all the women who are reading this book: your first indication that a man is not "the one," is if he pressures you to have sex. Know this, if you have sex with a man on the first date or, if you eventually give in to his desire for fear of losing him, you have already lost him. A man treasures a woman who treasures her virginity. A man will find it difficult to respect or fully trust a woman who is loose and easy to get with.

Let's open our Bibles and look in the Book of Proverbs. Take a glance at the warning signs of sexual impurity and the results of it.

Proverbs 2:11-19 NKJV Speaking on Wisdom and Understanding

Discretion will preserve you; Understanding will keep you, To deliver you from the way of evil, From the man who speaks perverse things, From those who leave the paths of uprightness, To walk in the ways of darkness; To deliver you from the immoral woman, From the seductress who flatters with her words, Who forsakes the companion of her youth, And forgets the covenant of her God. For her house leads down to death, and her paths to the dead; None who go to her return, Nor do they regain the paths of life.

Proverbs 5:3-6; 20 NKJV Beware of the immoral woman

For the lips of an immoral woman drip honey, And her mouth is smoother than oil; But in the end she is bitter as wormwood, Sharp as a two-edged sword. Her feet go down to death, Her steps lay hold of hell. Lest you ponder her path of life-- Her ways are unstable; You do not know them.

For why should you, my son, be enraptured by an immoral woman, And be embraced in the arms of a seductress?

Proverbs 5:21-23 NKJV The ways of a wicked man

For the ways of man are before the eyes of the Lord, And He ponders all his paths. His own iniquities entrap the wicked man, And he is caught in the cords of his sin. He shall die for lack of instruction, And in the greatness of his folly he shall go astray.

Proverbs 6:23-26 NKJV The Commandment

For the commandment is a lamp, And the law a light; Reproofs of instruction are the way of life, To keep you from the evil woman, From the flattering tongue of a seductress. Do not lust after her beauty in your heart, Nor let her allure you with her eyelids. For by means of a harlot a man is reduced to a crust of bread; And an adulteress will prey upon his precious life.

While you are living the single life, remain in a constant state of awareness of the immoral woman, the seductress, and the wicked man. The seductress is very crafty in her words and ways. She is stunning in her beauty. She is the trophy that men desire to have by their sides. But she has one purpose only and that is to lead you into sexual immorality and ultimately, separation from God. The wicked man is perverse in his thinking and his ways. He knows all of the right things to say to a woman, but his plans are evil. Your close relationship with God and seeking His wisdom will guard you from the trap of sexual immorality. This is why it is vitally important to accept His proposal and allow Him to lead you (men) or be led (women) to your perfect mate.

Women, beware that you don't become the immoral woman. The minute you agree to enter into sexual relations with a man you are not married to, you lead yourself and him into total damnation.

While you are single, you should be married only to Jesus. When you enter into a sexual relationship with someone who is not your spouse, you are not only committing fornication, but also adultery against your first love, Jesus himself.

Live your single life to the fullest. But also to the purest!

CHAPTER FOUR

The "PREP" Time

Esther 2: 12 NKJV "Each young woman's turn came to go in to King Ahasuerus after she had completed twelve months' preparation, according to the regulations for the women, for thus were the days of their preparation apportioned: six months with oil of myrrh, and six months with perfumes and preparations for beautifying women.

How do you prepare yourself for marriage? How do you know when you are ready? As I stated earlier; the right person at the wrong time, still makes the situation wrong. Since you cannot control when the right person will come, you must be prepared when the opportunity is presented.

The preparation time starts with a self-examination. The first question should be "How much of my soul does God control?" As you may know by now, marriage is a direct reflection of Jesus' relationship with the church. Before you prepare for marriage on earth, you should be perfecting your spiritual marriage to Jesus. Is He the Lord of your life? Do you seek Him in all things that you do? Is He a priority in your life? It has been said that the way you are in your relationship with Jesus is the way you will be with your marriage. Are you inconsistent in your prayer life? Do you expose your innermost thoughts to Him? Do you allow Him to make any decisions in your life? Do you honor Him by being obedient to His Word? Are you self-centered and depend only on you? All of these things will become a part of your marriage.

In your relationship with Jesus, you should always be in a state of humility, seeking to please Him more than yourself. You should have open and honest communication with Him, always knowing that you can be completely vulnerable with Him. In your time of preparation, check your level of commitment to the Lord. It is your commitment, trust, honesty and vulnerability that will prepare you to be a spouse.

Another thing to consider in your "prep time" is your single life. Have you fulfilled all that you desire to be as a single person? If not, how will these things affect you once you are married? The previous chapter mentions that if you wanted to pursue a college degree, start a business or travel, you should do these things now. Fulfill your personal dreams now or marry with the understanding that those things may not ever happen.

Remove the skeletons from your closet

We all have things in our past that we wish we could take back, do over, or just erase. We have done or experienced things that do not really reflect our true nature or character, those things that we never ever want anyone to know about like: being arrested, physical or sexual abuse, sexual promiscuity, abortion or drugs; the list goes on and on. The time to deal with and expose these things is right now, before you meet your potential mate. If you had a less than desirable childhood, broken relationship with your parents or siblings, all of these things need to be dealt with RIGHT NOW! Why is this so important? You want to offer your potential mate a whole person, a complete person without the pain of your past. You want to begin now to purify yourself by finding peace with anything that is or could become a skeleton in your closest. Again you may say, "Why?" Here's an example. An educated young lady with an established career meets a man and gets married. Life is good. They decide to have children but cannot. The doctor says the reason for it is the abortion she had five years earlier. This devastates her husband and the marriage because he never knew about the abortion, the skeleton in her closet. Because she never forgave herself, she withheld this information from him. Now this begins a long journey of distrust, hurt, pain and separation. He starts to question her integrity and the validity of other things in her past. Satan's desire is to use this to break up the marriage and kill the "happily ever after." Take your skeletons to God and as His Word says in 1 John 1:9, "If we confess our sins, He is faithful and just to forgive us of our sins and to cleanse us from all unrighteousness." Even if there was nothing you did but something done to you. Maybe you were sexually abused, or your parents abandoned you. Whatever created the skeleton in your closest, expose it to God and allow Him to purify and make you whole.

Just as God did with the children of Israel in the book of Deuteronomy, He brought them out of Egypt, out of a place of bondage. He was preparing to take them to the Promised Land, or in other words, the good life. Their journey was a time of purification, the "Prep Time." But before they could enter, they had to shake off their past, shake off the pains of bondage and slavery. They had to place their trust totally in God to love them, lead them, and take care of them. Most of all, they had to believe in Him. While you are in your "Prep Time," allow God to heal you of your broken and wounded past. If you have any skeletons that may haunt and destroy your future, defeat them now, long before you meet your potential "soul mate." Pray and get counseling from a spiritual leader or trained counselor. Remember, you cannot control the opportunity; you cannot control when this person will come across your path, but you can be prepared when they do.

Make yourself appealing to the opposite sex

Ladies

In 2006, a film based on the book of Esther was released called "One Night with the King." In the film it shows all of these beautiful virgin women preparing and hoping to have one night with the king. Listen to what it says about Esther.

> "She is taken in with the rest of the selected women and given cosmetics, perfumes, and treatments under the care of Hegai, the King's royal eunuch. Through her quick wit, intelligence and integrity, she becomes Hegai's favorite contestant. On their night with the king, the contestants are allowed to bring whatever they wished with them from the harem. They went in the evening and returned in the morning to a second harem to another royal eunuch who was custodian to the concubines. She would not be able to return to the king unless she pleased him and he summoned her by name. During their preparation, Hegai discovers Esther could read and listens to her reading to the other contestants. He admires her bravery, and stamina. Late into the night, he brings her to King Xerxes to read to him from the assigned scroll and [she] then begins telling him the love story of Jacob and Rachel (from the Old Testament). He is amused and intrigued and dismisses her, saying she would read to him again. From this interaction, Esther falls in love with the king. When Esther's turn comes for her 'one night with the king', she only wears what Hegai advises. She wins the

king's favor by revealing her heart to him. He chooses her and crowns her queen."

In this story, we see that the other women adorned themselves with make-up, much jewelry and clothing; all the things they thought were cute. Esther chose one simple necklace. It was because of her inner person that she found favor with Hegai. She receives his advice and wears only what he suggests, not what she thinks is cute. She wanted be appealing to the king, not herself. In the movie clip, what made Esther appealing to both the king and to the king's eunuch was her "quick wit, intelligence, integrity, her bravery and stamina." The king was both amused and intrigued by her. Esther was more concerned about preparing the inner person than the outer. She found out what was appealing to him rather than to herself or other women. There is absolutely nothing wrong with wearing jewelry, fine clothing, perfume, and dressing up the outer appearance, but if you want to be appealing to a real man, dress up the inner. 1 Peter 3:3-4 AMP says this, "Let not yours be the (merely) external adorning with (elaborate) interweaving and knotting of the hair, the wearing of jewelry, or changes of clothes; But let it be the inward adorning and beauty of the hidden person of the heart, with the incorruptible and unfading charm of a gentle and peaceful spirit, which (is anxious or wrought up) but is very precious in the sight of God."

Ladies, understand what a "real man" wants and become appealing in that way. You can attract a man with the outer, but it's the inner person that will keep him. Learn how to enhance your natural beauty without creating a whole new person. Place more emphasis on your inner beauty than on the outer. A man who falls in love with you and not your goods, is a man that will be there when the outer beauty starts to fade away.

Understanding what a "real man" wants is very simple, it's the same thing that God wants. Dress yourself up! Look like a woman, speak like a woman, act like a woman and you will attract a man. You can still be sexy without revealing all of your goods; yes it will attract a male, but not a man. A male will want to sex you, a man will want to get to know you and love you.

Men

In your "Prep Time," you too can gain a lot from this movie, "One Night with the King." In fact, it is in these types of movies that you can find a lot of information on how to attract and keep a good woman.

So men, what attracted Esther to the king? What made her fall in love with him? Some of you may reply, "He was a king. He was rich." Others may respond, "It is every little girl's dream to be a queen." Being a queen may have been a dream come true for Esther, but that is not what caused her to fall in love with the king. So men, what did she see in this man that you can learn from in your prep time? What made him so attractive? Let's start with the obvious: he was a wealthy and influential man. Being a man of financial substance is very attractive to a woman. It is in your financial stability that your potential spouse will find safety and security knowing that she can and will be provided for. Esther was not after wealth and riches; she was after the king's heart. On more than one occasion, the king offered Esther half of his kingdom but she did not accept his offer. So what does this mean to men during their prep time? No, it does not mean that you have to be wealthy or even rich. What it does mean is that you need to have some level of financial stability that shows your ability to provide a decent lifestyle for your bride.

What made the king attractive? He was a leader, well-spoken and capable of making major decisions. He was a man of integrity, honored and well respected by others. He was a man of power and authority. The most intriguing thing about the king as it relates to Esther is that he made her a priority in his life. This was evident because Esther was able to interrupt him at times when nobody else could. He was willing to lay aside his own personal agenda for that of Esther.

So again, what does this mean to you as a man during your prep time? Begin by being a man of character, one who knows his direction and purpose in his life. Be a man who honors God. Start now to put away the childish things and act like a man who already has the responsibility of a family. Have a long-term plan for your life, one that can include your future bride. Develop a reputation of integrity and honesty. Be a man whose character is spoken of highly by others.

Make yourself physically attractive. Dress yourself up, pull up your pants and drop the slang. The number one thing that attracts the type of woman that you want is a man who is well dressed, well groomed, articulate, and is a man of character. Keep your hair and nails neat and clean. Keep your facial hair neat and trimmed, your shoes polished and it does not hurt to smell good. Your appearance tells a woman a lot about you. If you are taking care of yourself physically, then you are probably taking care of yourself emotionally and financially. If you show some indication of being able to take care of yourself, then she will see your potential to take care of her.

Financial and Spiritual Preparation

Being financially sound and spiritually mature does not mean you have to be a priest with a lot of money. Before you move into the dating stage, you must be in a diligent pursuit of increased knowledge of the Word of God. You should be actively seeking wisdom, actively seeking understanding and actively pursuing God's plan for your life. While you are in this pursuit, you will find your most compatible person walking down the same pathway in pursuit of God's plan for their life.

As a man or a woman, being financially prepared for marriage is an absolute necessity. This does not mean you have to be rich or have a great job, have your own house or apartment. What it means is you must have a "proven" track record of being able to take care of yourself. What does this mean? You should have a clear vision for your life. You should have a written financial plan that includes a budget, strategic savings and emergency savings. As a man, understand now that it will be your responsibility to provide for your wife, and be prepared to do so. If your credit is bad, start now to repay your debt and repair your creditability. The same applies to a woman. If you have a trend of reckless spending and shopping, clean it up now before you meet someone. Ladies, you will find that a "real man" does not mind taking care of you financially. However, a man does not want to take on your out-of-control shopping and spending.

Prepare "The List"

Whenever you go to the grocery store to shop without a grocery list or a budget of what you want to spend, you will usually end up with things you did not intend to buy. You end up forgetting to purchase things that you needed and spending more than you intended. The same principal applies to preparing to meet, date and marry your spouse. So what am I saying? You NEED to dedicate some time to really knowing what it is that you want and need from your potential mate. More importantly, seek God for the things He wants for you in a mate. Who knows you better than you and God?

Between you and God, prepare a list of physical, spiritual, and mental attributes that you desire and would be comfortable with for the rest of your life. Why list the physical attributes? Because you know what is attractive to you. You do not want to meet, date or marry someone that you do not enjoy looking at. So men, your list might look like this: 5 feet, 7 inches, 155 pounds, short hair, long nails, big lips, small hips, athletic build. Someone else may prefer 5 feet, 10 inches, 195 pounds with long blonde hair and big legs. Women, the man of your dreams might be 6 feet, 2 inches, 220 pounds, dark hair, light eyes and muscular thighs. Whatever it is for you, close your eyes and without putting a familiar face on your ideal mate, daydream. Give a detailed description of what this person will look like.

When creating your list, consider such things as personality characteristics, moral and spiritual attributes, family dynamics, career desires, and thoughts on money, children, and religion. Your list should be as detailed and extensive as possible. This is not to say that you will find a person to match your list 100 percent, nevertheless, it will be your guide for knowing what is acceptable and what is not. Like the grocery list example, without the list, you may end up with things you didn't really want. You might also end up missing out on the things you really wanted. In the end, it could cost you much more than what you were willing to spend, that is the rest of your life in sorrow.

Ladies and gentlemen, take advantage of your singleness. Use this time to really prepare yourself for when that opportunity comes. Take the time to seriously understand what marriage is and how to have a successful one. The better prepared you are now, the better choices you will make. The better choices you make, the higher your chances are to have and enjoy a long-lasting marriage.

You don't practice when you get to the Super Bowl. You practice to get to the Super Bowl and WIN! The same applies to marriage; do not wait until you are married to prepare yourself or to try to make that person into your perfect mate. When you finally meet and choose to marry someone, be certain that there is no better match for you than the one you and God have chosen.

CHAPTER FIVE

MEET. DATE. MARRY?

2 Corinthians 6:14 GWT "Stop forming inappropriate relationships with unbelievers. Can right and wrong be partners? Can light have anything in common with darkness? Can Christ agree with the Devil? Can a believer share a life with an unbeliever?"

If you have not already made your list from the previous chapter, take some time now to do so. Once you have completed the list and are beginning to meet people, become intimate with that list yet not controlled by it. Allow God to speak and override your list. If the person does not match the physical desires on your list, do not be so quick to dismiss them. You will be surprised with how much more attractive a person will become when you get to know their character.

The meeting and dating process should not be a long drawn out process that takes months. If you have properly prepared your list, it can take you as little as a 30 minute phone conversation to say, "He is not the one." You must become resilient, not tough and rude or even soft and naive. Don't be so hard and harsh that people are afraid to talk to you. Likewise, don't be so gentle that people overlook your "no" and continue pursuing that which you clearly do not want. Although it may only take as little as 30 minutes to determine who is not, "the one," it could take months to figure how who is a good candidate. Be patient and allow God to lead you.

The Meeting

How do I meet people? How do I go about talking to someone that I might be interested in? How do I protect myself from being emotionally hurt or hurting someone else if the interest is not there?

The first rule of meeting is to do just that - meet. Never go into the meeting process with the thought of dating the person. You are truly just meeting the person. Do not make the mistake of meeting someone and within the first few conversations, thinking "this could be the one." You are not looking for someone, you are simply meeting someone. Without analyzing the person, you will know within a few minutes whether this could be someone you would like to continue conversing with. The only way you will truly know this is to become intimate with your list. Should you determine this is someone you may want to speak with again, be wise; do not give them your address or telephone number. If possible, don't even let them know where you work. The most discreet way of establishing a connection without committing to constant dialogue is through social media or email. Giving a person your email address sends a clear message that you control when, how, and if communication will exist. If you are truly not interested, do not blow them off by giving them your email address or any other contact information. If you have no plans to respond, do not leave them with that impression. A polite "it was nice meeting you" is very much appropriate.

Once you begin your email communication, learn as much as you possibly can by asking very pointed and direct questions.

Again, you are still meeting, yet discovering if there are any connections or things you have in common. Over time, you may develop a friendship that may lead to a less formal way of communication. You will find that some people you meet will have great conversation at first, but eventually it will fade away. Some will become "just people you know," some acquaintances and others may become friends. What is important here is that you give these relationships time to develop naturally without steering or manipulating them in a particular direction.

Also, as 2 Corinthians 6:14 says, do not form inappropriate relationships with unbelievers. In other words, your friends should be people who are like-minded in character and their spiritual beliefs. As a Christian, you cannot expect to build a healthy friendship with someone who does not believe in the same God you believe in. You cannot walk together with someone who is walking in a different direction. Choose your friends carefully and with advisement from those whom you know and trust.

Friendship does not mean you are now dating or that you will even get to the level of dating. Although that possibility does exist, it should not be your focus. Establish a clear understanding between you and your new friend that you are "just friends." This is so important because if it is not clear, it can cause friction when and if someone else comes along. As friends, you don't have to worry about making it clear that "we can date other people." A situation may come about that causes you and multiple "friends" to be in the same place at the same time. If you have the "friendship" understanding in place, no one should be uncomfortable.

While you are in the meeting and dating process, it is important to have a close friend to advise you along the way. This should be someone in whom you trust and knows you well.

They should be familiar with your likes and dislikes, your strengths and weaknesses. Do not allow the counsel of this friend to supersede that of your spiritual counsel. Remember, there is safety in a multitude of counsel, so surround yourself with like-minded people who can help you see beyond what's in front of you. Most importantly, invite the Holy Spirit to lead, guide and advise you as well. This is not the time to be vulnerable and emotionally intimate with people you are just meeting. Save the intimate and sacred details of your inner person. Once you have reached a point of serious relationship and you begin to discuss and discover each other, feel free to open up a bit more. It is only at the point of certainty when you know this is the one that you can completely open yourself up to. Why am I saying this? As human beings we all want to love and be loved. We want to know that someone is interested in us, understands us and cares for us.

Here is an example of this: it's a story of a mailman and an elderly woman. The woman was accustomed to being alone and having no one to talk with. Her husband of 40 years had recently passed and her closest relative was 1,200 miles away. Every day she would look forward to the mailman stopping by. Although he had heard the same stories told by her many times before, he would still take a minute to listen. After a few months, the widow began offering him a bottle of water. That eventually turned into a bottle of water and lunch. The mailman rarely talked about himself, he would just ask a general question and she would do all of the talking. During the holidays she would always give him gifts and a card. Finally, the day of her death came. The mailman found out through a neighbor who said, "Sorry to hear about your mom." Puzzled by the statement, the mailman said "Excuse me?" It was then that he learned the old woman had been telling the neighbors that he was her son. To the mailman, she was just another customer, but to her, he was a friend, a son. Most people are like this woman. It is not the fact that there is a person present to listen, but the feeling we get when we share ourselves with others. Don't be fooled by a person that appears to be interested in the inner you. Don't be so quick to share your world the first, second or third time you meet someone. When you do, pay close attention to how they respond and how much they open up and share with you.

Do your research

Most people will spend time researching what car to buy, the consumer rating on an appliance, or a school to send their children to. They will spend little to no time researching the people they get connected with. People will depend more on their emotions and feelings than on true knowledge of a person. In these days of the internet and social media, it is easy to find information on the general character of a person. You can find out who they are friends with, what they are interested in and how they spend their free time. You can even check to see if they have a criminal record. You should find out as much as possible about a person before you get connected to them. You can find out some things about them while you are communicating over the internet. However, do not be misled by what you might find on the internet; not everything is true, and some things may require an honest explanation. Always seek wisdom from God and guidance from the Holy Spirit.

Dating

This can and should be the fun time. You now have a general idea of the true character of this friend you are interested in dating. This can be a very awkward time because moving from friendship to dating can ruin the relationship. However, as a person interested in dating your friend, you must be open and honest with the person. When you develop feelings for a person you cannot expect them to know that you feel a certain way. Don't give subtle hints and expect them to figure it out. Be prepared to open up and tell them exactly what you are thinking. Also, be prepared to hear that they do not share the same feelings.

You may wonder, "How will I know?" You have probably heard people say "you'll just know." That is so very true. The key to this entire meeting, dating and marrying process is in the discussion from earlier chapters. First, develop a close relationship with God. He, along with the guidance of the Holy Spirit, will speak to your heart. He will give you warning signs when it's not right as well as when things are right. Second, prepare yourself. The right person may come along, however, you may not be prepared to receive them. Third is your list. At this point you are intimately familiar with the character attributes that you and God have created. If this friend closely matches what is on your list, you'll know. Finally, seek advice from those who know you best: your friends, family, your spiritual counselors and most of all God. They can help you see things that may not be so obvious to you. When all of these factors are in agreement, "you'll know."

Falling in Love

The feelings and emotions of being in love with someone can be intoxicating and deceiving. This is why the book begins with falling in love with Jesus. Allow that experience to be your roadmap of discerning between lust and love. This line between lust and love can be very thin and not always easy to distinguish. This is especially true with those whom you might meet or desire to date when that person is full of the love of God. Here's an example of what I'm speaking of: you find yourself attracted to a well-spoken Minister of the Word. He's single, you're single and it looks like the perfect situation. He's articulate, well-known and has a good reputation. Here is where it can be deceiving. You think that you are attracted to the person, when in reality, you are attracted to the anointing and the Spirit of God that rest upon that person's life. You'll find that you don't have anything in common with the person, but, because he is a Christian, you ignore all else and go for it. Now you both are on a road to destroying the anointing on his life and setting yourself up for a disappointing relationship.

The same holds true with two saved, sanctified, Holy Spirit-filled Christians. You both are on fire for God and love Him with all of your heart, mind and soul. You get together, yet you both have similar un-checked issues in your life. For instance, if you both still struggle with drugs or sex, you can guarantee that issues will arise and attempt to drive you into sin. One very important rule to follow is NEVER allow yourself to go on a date with this person alone. Always invite a friend that can and will maintain a sober mind and advise you accordingly. If you absolutely must meet alone, be sure that you drive separately and that you meet during the daylight in a very public place. Be sure that someone knows where you are going, when you get there and when you leave. This is not just for your emotional protection, but for your personal safety as well.

Marry?

Now that you have moved into the dating stage, marriage is a strong consideration but not a conclusion. You enter the dating stage with both parties having clear expectations and the understanding that dating "could" lead to marriage. Dating now becomes a time of deep discussion and really getting to know your friend on a more emotionally intimate level. It is a time to go beneath the surface of the person you have come to know. The times you spend together should be filled with conversation. Each person should open their door of vulnerability cautiously. It is okay to have fun while you are dating. Nevertheless, your goal should be on quickly determining if this person is someone that you want to marry. Is this someone who you can take orders from, submit to, and trust with your future?

While you are discussing the possibility of marriage, be sure to consider God's commandment to love. This commandment to love your spouse goes beyond your feelings and desires. It now becomes a commitment that you can no longer change. Once you say "I do," God expects you to do it His way. With that being the case, you better be certain that you can meet this commitment and this is the person that you can make it with.

Biblical Marriages

There are many love stories in the Bible that are worthy of reading and understanding while you are discussing marriage. During the early Bible days, marriages arranged by the parents were a standard practice. This was not God's original intention.

As we see with Adam and Eve, God did the arranging, yet Adam made the choice. God brought the woman to Adam, and it was Adam who said "this is now bone of my bones, and flesh of my flesh: she shall be called Woman, because she was taken out of Man." Genesis 2:23 NKJV. Adam recognized the importance of this woman to his life and God married them by saying, "Therefore shall a man leave his father and mother, and be joined to his wife, and they shall become one flesh."

Isaac and Rebekah – Here is another popular biblical love story that was an arranged marriage. Abraham, the father of Isaac, sent his servant on a journey to find a wife for Isaac. Abraham gave his servant instructions on where to go searching and told him that an Angel of the Lord will go before him to lead him to the woman. The Angel led the servant to a water well where he found Rebekah and other women working. You can read the story in its entirety in the book of Genesis chapter 24. Here are a few things I want to point out in this story. Isaac was about to become a wealthy man, he was set to inherit his father's fortune. This means he was financially capable of taking care of his bride long before he met her. The second thing I want to point out is with Rebekah. When the Angel of the Lord led the servant to her, he found her working. Let's look at how the Bible describes Rebekah's character. The Amplified Bible (Genesis 24:16), describes her as beautiful, attractive, chaste, modest and unmarried. This is a very interesting description of Rebekah because at the time of this description, Rebekah was headed to the well to draw water. In other words, she was working. It is likely that she was not wearing heels, a tight skirt and a low cut blouse, yet she is described as attractive. Verses 17 through 20, describe how she responded to this stranger's request. It says she "quickly let down her jar" and she "ran again to the well." Her actions speak of her character as being one of a gentle and kind nature, not lazy, willing to be a servant. This is just the kind of woman a man looks for.

The final thing I want to point out in this love story is that Abraham and his servant trusted that God would lead them to a wife for Isaac. Even with Abraham trusting in God, he knew that the woman still had the choice to go with him (Genesis 24:8). We know that in verses 57 and 58, Rebekah decides to go. As Rebekah and Abraham's servant arrived, they found Isaac praying and as he rose up from praying, he saw the camels coming. Upon one of the camels was Rebekah, and it was love at first sight. What is interesting about this encounter was the very first time Rebekah laid eyes upon Isaac, she saw him praying. This was probably an instant attraction for her as most women desire this attribute in a husband. This was a marriage arranged by God. All of the pieces were already in place to make for a successful marriage.

The story of Isaac and Rebekah is a fascinating story that I recommend you read while reading this book. Another fascinating love story is found in the book of Ruth. Similar to Isaac and Rebekah, Boaz was a very wealthy man and he found his bride working. Both of these women displayed the characteristics of a gentle and meek spirit, willing to serve. Both of the men were able to take good care of the women they chose to be their brides. Most of all, both couples were led by God and the marriages were arranged by God.

I ended the chapter with these stories to illustrate the importance of being sure your character is one that God can use before you meet, date, and marry someone. Be sure your heart is right. God will send you down the path of meeting your perfect mate, but you must be willing to allow Him to lead you. Only you and God can make the final decision on whether this is the right person and the right time. Follow His leading and those whom He has placed in your life to advise you. Be sure you're sure, because divorce is NOT an option!

CHAPTER SIX

IF YOU WANT IT,
PUT A RING ON IT.

Ephesians 5: 15-17 NKJV "See then that you walk circumspectly, not as fools but as wise, redeeming the time, because the days are evil. Therefore do not be unwise, but understand what the will of the Lord is."

James 5:12 NKJV "But above all, my brethren, do not swear, either by heaven or by earth, or with any other oath. But let your "Yes" be yes and your "No" be no. Lest you fall into judgment."

Even in a relationship arranged by God we are still given the choice to marry or not. From the beginning God gave us free will and the right to choose every aspect of our lives. Choosing who to marry and when, is an important decision to make. Take your time but don't waste your time. You will never learn all there is to know about a person, so once you have learned enough - move on!

At the point of dating a person you should have already established open and honest communication. Do not allow the person to be misled. If you know that the two of you are not thinking the same thoughts, then make it clear. Do not withhold your feelings and opinions for fear of hurting them. It's best to keep the lines of communication open to prevent hurt feelings and misunderstandings later. Don't drag out the dating game knowing that you are truly not interested in going any further. Sure, you may enjoy being with the person, hanging out and talking all night. But if you know in your heart that anything more than a friendship would never work, make your feelings known as soon as possible and seek the wisdom of God on how to express them. Once you have communicated your desire to move on, you can no longer maintain the same level of relationship. The going out, and talking all night has to come to a complete halt. If not, you may mislead the person into thinking it's not really over.

If you are proposing or being proposed to, it should not come as a surprise. Men, when you drop down on one knee and present her with that ring, you should KNOW that she is going to say "yes." The time, the place, and the romance should all be a surprise, but not the fact that you are proposing. Movies and romance novels have convinced us that these fairy tale proposals are real. The writers of these stories know for certain that she will say yes and so should you.

Remember, "Right person, wrong time." You can destroy a potentially good relationship by proposing at the wrong time. Men, if she said she does not want to marry until she finishes school, don't propose to her in her senior year. Ladies, if he said he is not ready until all of his debt is paid, then don't pressure or guilt him into a proposal. The proposal should come at a time when both are ready for marriage. A proposal too early will usually result in a lengthy engagement. What happens is one or both parties try to complete their list of "things to do before I get married" while they are engaged. The engagement, wedding planning, life planning and honeymoon planning all end up competing with one another and cause stress and confusion. As I stated in the "Livin' Single" chapter, complete everything you planned to complete while you are single. If you have made a conscious decision to move on without completing something, it should never rise again unless both of you agree.

Premature Engagement

There is a movie called "The Five Year Engagement." It is about a young couple who loved each other and really enjoyed being together. By all accounts Tom and Violet were truly meant to be together. He proposed, she accepted and there began their journey of engagement. Both of them had individual career aspirations that they had not accomplished. Tom wanted to become a head chef at a restaurant and Violet wanted to continue her studies in psychology. A series of events caused them to delay their wedding several times. Finally, Tom set aside his aspirations to support Violet. He eventually grew increasingly resentful towards Violet as she lived out her desires. Their frustration with each other caused them to grow apart. Violet fell for another man, Tom's anger drove him to someone he really did not like and the engagement was called off. According to the norm in romance movies they eventually linked back up after a few years and had the fairytale wedding.

This movie is interesting because there is a huge lesson to be learned about preparing for marriage at the point of engagement. Unfortunately life does not work like the movies. In most cases, after breaking up and returning the ring, one or both parties are no longer interested in the other. Once you have determined that "this could be the one," the very next step is counseling.

Pre-marital Counseling

During your discussions on marriage, you should talk about every aspect of your lives, your likes, dislikes, wants, needs and desires. Find books and on-line teachings on marriage to study and discuss. This is not a marriage planning session, however, it is very important to know and make known what you expect from your potential spouse. Take some time to daydream together and daydream apart. Make note of the things you come up with and discuss them. Once you have thoroughly discussed marriage with one another, make an appointment with a marriage counselor. This date will be more important than your wedding date. Pre-engagement or post-engagement, seek spiritual, professional marriage counseling. It is probably best that you pursue pre-engagement counseling. Not that there are two different types of counseling, but pre-engagement can help you prepare for the engagement. Pre-engagement counseling comes from close friends and relatives that you have given some spiritual authority in your life. Pre-marital counseling with a trusted, ordained minister or licensed professional will help you discover things you've never talked about or thought about. The more things you discover and discuss now, the better off you will be once you are married.

What are you trying to accomplish in pre-marital counseling? There are two things you need to determine: your compatibility and readiness. Just because the two of you love spending time together, this does not mean you will be compatible. You may be better off as friends than as lovers. Be sure to find a counselor that will conduct an extensive discovery of your history. Many times events in your history and family traditions help to shape your beliefs and behaviors without you knowing it. Simple things like who carves the turkey at

Thanksgiving can turn into a major disagreement. A reminder of a traumatic event during your childhood can trigger an emotion that will attack your marriage. A skilled and trained counselor can help you search beneath the surface and expose a problem before it occurs. He or she can help you see where you are compatible and discover areas that might present a problem.

The thought or feeling of being in love can sometimes blind you of the obvious. You could go on thinking that you and your potential mate are ready to take your relationship to the next level. A skilled counselor can detect if the timing is right or if you need to wait. Remember you are discussing a lifelong commitment that cannot be changed, so it is best seek wisdom and to follow their advice.

How will I know?

How will I know I'm ready to propose? How can I be certain that I'm ready to say yes? There are two ways:

1) Be spiritual. Check your inward witness for the peace of God. Are you totally and completely under the authority of the Word of God? Can you follow God's instructions without hesitation? Is there any pride or selfishness in you?

2) Be realistic. Are you financially stable enough to handle marriage? Are you emotionally stable enough to handle marriage? Do you have any hidden issues that might creep up in your marriage? Have you closed the door on past relationships? Have you gotten control of any "baby mama/daddy drama" that could reap havoc in your relationship? All of these things should be introduced and dealt with during your pre-marital counseling. Love can be intoxicating. Take a minute to step

49

down from your cloud of love and become sober in your thinking. Only you will truly know if you are ready, and if you are not, be honest about it.

Ready to put a ring on it

The wedding ring is a symbol of your commitment to one another. It is a physical, tangible expression of your love. Neither the size of the diamond, nor the cost should determine your commitment to love, so be practical. Make the decision together by considering your current financial state and your future plans. If you truly love one another the way God loves you, then you will never find a diamond big enough. Men, do not be afraid to discuss cost before you begin looking at any ring. Do not set yourself up or set a false expectation for your potential fiancée. If you find that you cannot afford exactly what you want right now, then plan to upgrade on a milestone anniversary. Don't create and carry debt into your marriage without knowing or having a plan and the ability to pay it off.

Let your "yes" be "yes" and your "no" be "no." If you are not 100 percent certain that this is the person you want to spend the rest of your life with then, say no. If the timing is not right, then "not now," is very much appropriate. If you are sure, do not waste time; if you want it, put a ring on it!

CHAPTER SEVEN

Married with Children

> Luke 14:28 NKJV "For which of you, intending to build a tower, does not first sit down and count the cost, whether he has enough to finish it?"

You are not even married yet and already talking about having children, buying a house, and furniture. That is because getting married is more than just a wedding ceremony, the honeymoon and living happily ever after. It is about building a life together, daydreaming, planning, and living life to the fullest. There is a lot to consider between the "I do" and the "happily ever after." This chapter will provoke you to think about the cost of having the marriage you really want. The time to think and plan is before you say "I do."

Many couples put a lot of effort into planning the wedding and honeymoon. They spend hours upon hours looking for the perfect dress, choosing the wedding cake, sending out invitations, and the list goes on. A wedding is a major task and it can be extremely stressful. Because of the amount of work involved in planning a wedding, couples will usually hire a wedding planner. The cost can range from $1,500 to $10,000 or more depending on the services they provide. In addition to the fees you pay to the wedding planner, the average cost of a wedding is approximately $27,000. Some of you may be blessed to have someone else to pay for your wedding. In spite of this, you should still consider how to best utilize these financial resources. Consider how much should be used for the wedding and how much can be used to plan your life together.

You've said "I do," had the first dance, honeymooned in Hawaii, and now you're home. You have reminisced about the wedding, looked at the pictures a thousand times, put away the wedding gifts, and packed up the wedding dress. This is usually the beginning of a silent spiral downward as your fantasy collides with reality. "I'm married, now what?" Sure the newlywed phase will float you on a cloud for a few more months, but you will soon get those subtle hints of reality. "I'm really married!" You see clearly that this perfect person you just married is far from perfect. Then there are the real expenses of being married that come at you like a freight train with no brakes. To avoid the newlywed breakdown, here are a few things that a couple should consider prior to the "I do."

Where are we going to live?

Determining where you are going to build a life together is an exciting time. Yet, it can also be very stressful. Discussing where you are going to live is vital before you marry. Many times the bride has one thought and the groom has a different thought. One person may want to live close to family and friends and the other wants to live far away. These decisions can be a deal breaker in the decision to marry, and that is completely okay. It is best to find out before committing than to have a melt down after you are married. Decide as a couple if the place you have chosen is a long term decision and if you move, under what circumstances would you move. Have a very detailed discussion; talk about the type of home you like. Will it be a house or apartment? What area of town, how many bedrooms and most of all, how much are you able to afford? One or both of you may already have a home and it may be best to move out of those homes and into a place chosen together. The options are limitless. The point is that you come to a decision together.

How many children do we want to have?

Having children is a blessing from the Lord. They are precious and rewarding gifts from God. You and your potential mate may already have children from previous relationships. Discussing the dynamics of raising the children you have, and how many children you want to have together will save you a ton of heartache and pain. Having children can be very costly, especially when you want to provide only the best for them. If you are like most parents, you do not want to see your children go without anything. So when deciding if you will have children and how many, consider the long-term expense of providing for them. Consider things like a college fund, private school or public school or home schooling. You must think about the cost of clothing, birthdays, Christmas, extra-curricular activities and unexpected events, or medical expenses.

Proverbs 13:22 tells us that a good man leaves an inheritance for his children's children. So in your consideration of having children, you must plan now for your grandchildren as well. You cannot plan for everything but, without a plan you are likely to be surprised by one or two events that could destroy your marriage. Here's a scenario of what usually happens. You drive up in your $50,000 BMW carrying your $400 purse and the Little League coach asks you for $100 for new uniforms. You are too prideful and embarrassed to say you cannot afford it, so you put more stress on your finances to make it happen. That stress from your finances spills over into your marriage, which spills over into your children. Divorce happens and the child now wonders if he was the cause of it. This may seem simple and ludicrous however, this very case happens all of the time.

Who is going to handle the money?

The money issue is one that attacks newlyweds in a silent, but deadly way. Hiding behind a loving smile is the question of trust. "I love you. I just don't trust you with my money." It is a common theme in most households for there to be separate accounts. Each party wants to control their own money to keep down arguments and disagreements. They settle in to their marriages with the dysfunction of non-verbal disagreement that says my way is better than yours. Some say that the man is the head of the house so he should handle the finances. Others say that the woman is better organized so she should be the one. "You pay the mortgage and I'll pay the car note." It sounds good but it goes completely against the biblical model of marriage.

Remember this chapter was written to provoke thought and conversation with your potential mate. Making these decisions now will avoid a lot of headache and disappointments in the future. So, who should handle the money? It really does not matter who takes on the responsibility of executing the "joint" decision of where the finances will go. The important thing is that both parties are involved and making decisions together. Having separate accounts, making major purchases without the other person, and stashing money all will attack your unity. An attack on the unity of marriage will open the door to other separations and eventually destroy your marriage. The marriage was built on the principle of unity; that is total oneness. Separate accounts of any kind promotes both pride and selfishness, neither of which have any room in marriage. There are a select few cases where separate accounts can be advantageous, however, both parties should have complete and total access to those accounts. Not only should both have access, but both should have the ability to make decisions concerning them.

Life Insurance and Financial Planning

This is the area that usually goes unnoticed until it is too late. Consider something as simple as the air conditioning unit going out or the engine on your car stops working. There are always major events in the life of a couple that they can be prepared for and others come as a surprise. Think about the things that you know you want to do then create a financial plan to support it. Consider things such as having children, college funds, purchasing a house, retirement, a dream vacation. Then plan for the unexpected such as house or car repairs. Consider a life insurance policy in the event something happens to you and the other is left with one income to take care of the children.

Many newlyweds think that they don't make enough money to have a financial planner. This is far from the truth. Most banks and financial institutions have trained financial advisors that can help you establish credit, repair credit and create a financial plan to support the things you want to do now and in the future.

Vacations and recreation

Vacate the day-to-day stresses and concerns of life. Get away and re-create love and passion for each other. Create memorable moments for the kids that they will want to duplicate when they become parents. As an engaged couple, daydream together. Talk about things you would like to do, places you would like to go. Talk, talk, talk! The purpose of this book and specifically this chapter is to prepare you for marriage and get you to think about life after the honeymoon. Consider the value of cherished memories and creating special moments with the kids that will last forever. The value of doing these things now, will completely outweigh the expense. Creating memories does not always have to cost you money but certainly your time and energy.

Expectations in communications

"Communications of expectations results in transformations of relations and creations of aspirations therefore no domination in the cohabitation of said relations."

When you're in love, you hear a statement like that and perhaps think, "yeah, that was deep." When you come down off of the cloud, it's like "WHAT?" Something was said but nothing was understood. We all have expectations from those we communicate with. We know what we expect to give and what we expect to receive. The problem is, does the other person know? "Well, I told them." Telling a person does not always mean understanding took place. Therefore, you may find yourself repeating and repeating and repeating until understanding takes place. One of the most valuable questions you can ask is "what do you mean by that?" Communication problems are among the top reasons given for divorce. Make it a point now to create an environment where open and honest communications can take place. Give grace to each other when a failure in understanding or in communication takes place. Begin discussing now what you expect from one another. Investing in clear and concise communications during your engagement will yield a return of a strong loving relationship after you are married.

In EVERY circumstance mentioned above, you must first consult God in prayer. Also, commit to open, honest and timely communication. Lastly, make a plan, get it on paper and pray over it daily. Lack of planning could prove to be disastrous and cause unnecessary stress on your marriage.

Before you accept or make the proposal, count the cost. Consider every aspect of being married. Discuss having children and how many. Talk about the type of lifestyle you want to live.

The Marriage Counselor

When you consider all of those who you have to pay after the wedding: the photographer, caterer, the DJ, and the limo driver, at the bottom of the list you might find the Officiator and Marriage Counselor. Those who are most valuable are the least considered and the least paid. A Marriage Counselor can help you see the whole movie at one time and not just scene by scene. According to divorce.org, the divorce rate among Americans ranges from 40 to 50 percent in the United States. It would appear that Marriage Counselors would be at the top of the list of those getting paid. The truth is couples rarely see or consider the value in having someone help them prepare for their marriage, therefore, a large percentage of them end in divorce.

In your preparation for marriage, pre-marital counseling is a must. Think of it like breathing, you cannot exist without it. The ideal thing to do is to seek a counselor that will be with you before, during, and after the wedding. Consider having frequent "tune-up" meetings with him or her. Allow them to walk you through some of life's tough moments that you are guaranteed to experience.

Make a plan. Build into your plan contingencies for life's interruptions. We all know that life never goes as planned, but this does not mean to not plan at all. It means be flexible in your planning. Give God the power and influence over your plan and allow Him to guide you through the changes.

Marriage is a great thing! God wants you to have and enjoy your marriage to the fullest. It is in the center of His heart for you to love and be loved. So in your consideration of marriage, count the cost.

Sources:
http://weddings.costhelper.com/wedding-planner.html
http://wedding.theknot.com/wedding-planning/wedding-budget/qa/what-does-the-average-wedding-cost.aspx

CHAPTER EIGHT

MONSTER-IN-LAW

Romans 12:18 NKJV "If it is possible, as much as depends on you, live peaceably with all men."

When you make the decision to date someone or even marry, you are instantly connected with those closest to him/her. Like it or not, these people will play a large role in your relationship. As the saying goes, "you can choose your friends but not your family." However, you can choose the family and friends you associate with and allow to have influence in your life. More importantly, you are in control of how you relate to them. This means you get to choose how you respond to any negativity from these relationships. This will become extremely helpful to you during the dating process and even more once you are married.

Friends and relatives can be a great indicator of the true character of the person you are dating. Don't be so quick to dismiss or disassociate yourself from the friends of your potential mate. Invite them into your circle as you get to know your potential mate. These people can provide you with very valuable insight to how your future might be with them. Be wise, and remember everything you hear may not be the truth so always seek God for discernment.

Keep this in mind, in her/his circle of friends, you are the "new kid on the block." Her girlfriend, his mother, her brothers, and/or his sisters, have been there long before you were even thought of. They will know your potential mate better than you and will have more influence. In most cases, some of these people will have a more intimate relationship with her/him simply because of the history they share. This is not something to be intimidated by because it can be an opportunity to discover more about her/him from a third party.

So how do you handle the best friend who appears to be a negative influence? How do you handle the mother-in-law who treats her son like he is still a baby? How do you deal with the ex-girlfriend who is a friend of the family and still cares for the man you are now dating? There are many dynamics to friends and relatives that need deep discussion while you are dating. You will never get rid of Mom and you can't ask your "groom-to-be," to throw away twenty years of friendship with "his boy." So what do you do? There are thousands of scenarios that can creep up to cause a disruption in your desire to marry. There are no clear or simple answers on what to do. There are some things you should consider, discuss, and agree upon prior to committing to marriage. You can discuss and agree on a plan for how to handle a friend or relative should a problem arise. It is your commitment to each other that will get you past the problems and issues.

It is important to know that trying to get your potential mate to change her/his friends is equivalent to trying to change them. It will never work and it will prove damaging to your relationship. You will begin to build an invisible wall of resentment that will eventually appear once you settle into marriage. You should first validate your feelings by consulting your spiritual mentor or discuss it in counseling. Be sure you are not being judgmental or selfish in your opinion of the friend or relative. By now you should have a strong relationship with your potential mate that allows you to discuss your feelings freely. Remember, you are not asking him or her to change friends but simply expressing your feelings. The decision to make a change of any kind is totally up to her/him. The ownership of how to deal with the change or decision not to change will rest completely upon your shoulders. In some cases this could be a game-changer. You may decide that his drug-dealing best friend is not a relationship you are willing to tolerate. You cannot control the ex-girlfriend who still has feelings for him, nor can you control her relationship with his family. What you can do is set boundaries to protect your relationship and control how you respond to situations that you cannot avoid.

The In-Laws

We have all heard stories about the over-protective father-in-law who threatens the potential son-in-law and the "monster-in-law" who thinks there is no one good enough for her son. Getting off on the wrong foot with the in-laws is one of the biggest mistakes a newlywed couple can make. The issues usually begin with simple things done unintentionally, yet resulting in major relationship and communication breakdowns. Relationships with in-laws must be handled with delicate hearts and a sensitive, controlled tongue. In every situation you are the "outsider" trying to merge into a history of strong relational ties. The effort of building a relationship with your potential in-laws will fall on you. That may not be an easy task. You may never go shopping with your mother-in-law, or go fishing with your father-in-law. In spite of that, you can find a place of mutual agreement and understanding that promotes peace for all. Don't try to be the person they want you to be by conforming to their every request. Respect them, honor them for the role they play in your marriage, but be who God created you to be.

Do not go into a marriage knowing that there are issues with in-laws that need to be addressed yet you fail to do so. Once you are married, the whole relationship dynamic changes. Your husband/wife and your marriage will become the highest priority in your life next to God. When it comes to your family, friends, mother, father and siblings, they all take a backseat to your spouse. You should make every effort to support your spouse in disagreements or conflicts that will come up. As a husband or a wife, your responsibility is not to take sides in a conflict but to seek righteousness, joy and peace in every situation. Under no circumstances should you ever allow your spouse to be spoken of or spoken to in a demeaning or disgraceful way. Be careful not to dishonor them by doing so yourself.

This subject of friends and relatives is a very sensitive subject that, if not handled properly, can destroy a good thing. The way you start with these relationships will set the tone for how you relate to them in the future. You can only control you, so always be willing to extend mercy, kindness and initiate reconciliation when needed. Be the Christian; live the Word of God in all situations regardless of the actions of others.

Here are a few simple rules related to friendship for married couples:

If he/she cannot be friends of both the husband and wife, they have no place in your life, especially if they are of the opposite sex.

The term "friend," in this case, refers to someone close to you. A friend is a person that you communicate with often and has some influence in your life. They are people that you can confide in and lean on for advice. Here is how you can tell a true friend: a true friend will never support you in wrong doing. They will always give advice that promotes and protects the sanctity of marriage. A true friend will help you to focus on the good and will always point you to the Word of God and to a place of righteousness. The "friend" may be closer to one than the other, but both the husband and wife should be able to call them a friend. If this friend is not married, and/or non-spiritual, they have no advice to offer you concerning your relationship.

Some friends are friends for life and others are for a season. It is completely okay to have friends who are not married and who are non-spiritual. The key is to understand the role they play in your married life. Marriage is a spiritual institution created by God. If your friend is non-spiritual, they are not qualified to give you spiritual marital advice. This does not mean they don't have good intentions, they simply lack understanding. This could also be the case with a married friend with no understanding; inviting their opinion on your marriage can prove to be a major mistake. It would be like having a plumber do a root canal. Be careful who you allow to give you any advice concerning your marriage.

If intimate details of your sexual relationship are to be discussed, they must not be discussed with friends. This level of conversation should only be done with a spiritual Christian or Professional Marriage Counselor. Be aware that many cases of husbands/wives having affairs with their spouse's best friend are a result of visual images placed in their minds based on statements made by the spouse. You could be the person who turned the friend on to your spouse! Watch your words.

Always seek spiritual counsel. Look for a couple who can serve as both counselors and mentors to your marriage. This couple must be a couple who not only knows the Word but also exemplifies it in their own lives.

Here's a simple rule on family relations and the married couple:

Keep family out of your business. Although they may really mean well, it can sometimes be difficult for them to have an unbiased opinion. Gossip about your marriage can spread faster within the family and often faster than with friends. The only exception to this is if both the husband and wife agree that the family member is capable of providing wise, godly counsel.

Remember this, when you are dealing with family, friends, and other relationships, you are in control of your responses, your actions, and reactions. No one can make you happy, mad or angry unless you give them permission to do so. When you do respond, your response should always promote love, peace, and joy which is righteousness.

CHAPTER NINE

DIVORCE IS NOT AN OPTION

Genesis 2:24 NIV "For this reason a man will leave his father and mother and be united to his wife, and they will become one flesh."

"Divorce is not an option." A very well-known Hollywood couple coined this phrase years ago. It is the same view that God had when He created the institution of marriage. To hear this coming from a Hollywood couple came as a complete surprise and raised the public's level of respect for them. Unfortunately, a few years later, the couple who had publicly declared "divorce is not an option," determined that it was their only option.

Divorce is NOT an option. This statement holds so much value and truth, yet it lacks understanding and application in marriages today. This chapter is probably the single most important chapter in this book. If you are reading this, my guess is that you have a desire to marry at some point in your life. If this is the case, the information in this chapter is of vital importance to you as you prepare to date your soul mate. Couples rarely go into a marriage planning to get a divorce. It is their lack of understanding, lack of commitment to God's way and lack of preparation which leads them in that direction when they feel they have no other choice.

Through the eyes of the author

A while back, I attended two weddings in the same year. Both were beautiful ceremonies and the couples seemed so in love and happy to be married. At the reception of one, my wife and I huddled up with the giddy newlyweds and confessed these words over them, "divorce is not an option." They smiled in agreement and said "that's right." Six months later they were separated and divorced.

In the other wedding, I sat and watched as the beautiful bride strolled down the aisle with her father by her side. She smiled at me as though to say, "I've been waiting for this day for a long time." As she approached the altar to meet her groom, her best friends stood waiting to support her and his best friends were there supporting him. In the background were hundreds of friends, family members, and co-workers. As they stood anxiously waiting to be married, the minister began to speak these words: "Dearly beloved, we are gathered here in the sight of God, and in the face of this company..." It was right there that it hit me. My focus and attention intensified on the bride, the groom and all those present. I realized at that very moment that neither the bride nor groom "really" understood what was about to happen. Looking into the audience, I also realized that we were not just guests, but now witnesses to the commitment these people were making to each other and to God. Thanks to God, they are happily married to this day. This experience revealed to me our lack of true understanding of marriage vows and the commitment being made to God.

The Ceremony

Marriage ceremonies have become routine. Reverence for God and His commandments concerning marriage are often lost. Couples are so captured by the moment, they do more thinking than listening to what the minister is saying. The groom is thinking about the honeymoon and the bride is fighting off tears to keep her makeup from running. They hear the minister speaking, yet they do not comprehend what he really means. So what is this minister saying and what does it really mean? What is this couple agreeing to when they say "I do" and "I will?" Below is a script from a traditional marriage service. This script is not used in every ceremony, however, the foundation is pretty much the same. The point in giving you this example is not for you to study it, but to provoke your thinking about your vows and what you are committing to.

> Dearly beloved, we are gathered together here in the sight of God, and in the face of this company, to join together this man and this woman in holy matrimony...

The word "holy" used in the ceremony is referring to God's view and original plan for marriage. It is sacred, special, and so dear to God that not only is He present (in the sight of God), but He is a part of the union and the One who created the institution. The guests are not there for the sole purpose of bearing gifts and well wishes, they serve as witnesses to this commitment.

> ...which is an honorable estate, instituted of God, signifying unto us the mystical union that is betwixt Christ and His church...

God looks upon marriage with joy because He sees what He has created being duplicated between the groom and his bride. The word mystical does not refer to something mysterious or spooky. It refers to the mystery that has been revealed, the relationship of Christ and the church. In other words this union between a man and a woman is a direct reflection of the marriage between Christ and the church.

> ...which holy estate Christ adorned and beautified with His presence and first miracle that He wrought in Cana of Galilee. And is commended of Saint Paul to be honorable among all; and therefore is not by any to be entered into unadvisedly or lightly; but reverently, discreetly, soberly, and in the fear of God.

This statement is still a part of the opening statement and is not only addressing the couple, but all who are present. This sort of "warning statement" is a reminder of the sanctity and holiness of marriage. Marriage should not be entered into without receiving advice, which is pre-marital counseling. It should be entered into reverently and with discretion; this means having the power or right to decide or act according to one's own judgment; freedom of judgment or choice.

Soberly, in this case does not mean sober from drinking or intoxication, although that is included. Many times a couple can be so in love with the thought of being in love and being married that they are not acting from a clear, conscious state of mind. Stress, hurt, pain, disappointment, and anger can all drive you into intoxicating, non-sober decisions. Joy, excitement, lust and pseudo-love can be equally as intoxicating. Many people jump into marriage after the death of a loved one, a divorce or some other tragedy, times when they are most vulnerable. Some unknowingly use marriage as a Band-Aid to cover and pacify those pains. This is why it is so important to have a counselor who can filter through all of the reasons you want to marry and help you decide if it is the right thing to do as well as the right time to do it.

"In the fear of God" means this is higher than your respect for your parents, higher than your respect for the law and higher than your respect for those in authority. Fear or reverence for God's law and plan for marriage is your highest consideration before saying "I do." God's original intention and plan was written at the point of instituting marriage. This plan is found in Genesis 2:24 (NKJV) saying, "Therefore a man shall leave his father and mother and be joined to his wife, and they shall become one flesh." These words "joined" and "one flesh" are permanent, never to be separated. God no longer looks upon the man and the woman as two individuals but as one. Only God can make them one; therefore only God can make them two again, so in the eyes of God, divorce is not an option.

> Into this holy estate these two persons present come now to be joined. If anyone can show just cause why they may not lawfully be joined together, let him now speak, or else hereafter forever hold his peace.

As I stated earlier, all who are present for this wedding are not just guests, but they are active participants, witnesses. If you have "just cause" does not mean this is the time to speak out and cause a scene during this "holy" time. "Just cause" does not mean just 'cause you don't like it or because one or both parties are living in sin. If you have strong feelings for why this couple should not marry, the time to make your feelings known is before the wedding. Your feelings may in fact be legitimate, yet, that does not stop the couple from being married. If the couple decides to continue with their wedding plans after your feelings have been made known, it's probably best that you decline the invitation to participate. There are only few "just cause" reasons that should be addressed when the presiding minister makes this statement. One reason is one party or the other is attempting to defraud the other by marrying under false pretenses. There are at least two reasons that go against God's law of marriage; 1) One or both parties are already married, 2) The couple is of the same sex. Even if these situations are true, it is still best to address it before the ceremony and not during.

Now speaking to the couple about to be married, the minister will say;

> I require and charge you both, as ye will answer at the dreadful day of judgment when the secrets of all hearts shall be disclosed...

This statement is a preparatory statement for what is to follow. What is basically being said here is "I'm telling you both to be honest with your response to this next statement, because the day will come when you meet God face-to-face and the truth will be revealed and dealt with."

He continues by saying:

> ...that if either of you know of any impediment, why ye may not be lawfully joined together in matrimony, ye do now confess it.

In other words, the first time I was speaking to all witnesses present, now I am addressing you both directly. If you know of any reasons why you should not be married, confess it now. Why confess it now? Because of the next line that follows:

For be well assured, that if any persons are joined together otherwise than as God's Word doth allow, their marriage is not lawful.

So you may continue with the ceremony, but if there is anything that goes against God's law, the marriage is not lawful in the sight of God. The law of the land may say that it is legal, yet God will not acknowledge it.

Now to the vows

Speaking to the man first and then the woman, the minister shall say:

_____ wilt thou have this woman/man to be thy wedded wife/husband, to live together after God's ordinance in the holy estate of matrimony? In other words, will you have this person now as a part of you; as one flesh living together, loving together and growing together as one according to God's law, His plan and His design for marriage?

Wilt thou love her/him, honor and keep her/him in sickness and in health; forsaking all others, keep thee only unto her/him, so long as you both shall live?

The typical and expected response to this question is "Yes" or "I will." Most of the time couples respond with the expected answer not knowing what they are committing to. When you respond with "yes" or "I will," what you are really saying is this: "As long as I am breathing and have life in my body, I commit to love her/him." This love you are committing to is not just an affectionate love (storge), not just a brotherly love (philo), not just an erotic love (eros), it is a commanded love, God's way of loving, which is agape, unconditional, without limits or terms of agreement. You cannot follow a command unless you have first given the person issuing the command authority in your life. If God is not an authority figure in your life, His commands mean nothing to you. Secondly, it is impossible to love someone unconditionally without first having the love of God inside you. If you answer "yes," or "I will," without having God as the commander of your life and without having God's love in you, God will still accept your answer, and He will expect you to live by it as well.

Your answer also comes with the understanding that as long as you both are living, you will honor and keep each other both when you are healthy and in the event of sickness/terminal illness. This honor that you are committing to is one of high esteem and regard. It means you are promising to maintain a good name and reputation at all times. All that you are and all that you do now has an impact on the person you are marrying. You must never do anything to bring shame or embarrassment to your spouse.

"Forsaking all others..." means that next to your relationship with God, your wife/husband is the most important person in your life. You are vowing that everyone and everything else will take a backseat to your spouse. This includes parents, children, and church. "Keep thee only unto her/him, so long as you both shall live" simply put, means your spouse is the only authorized recipient of your sexual expression: keep it that way! Now remember this, these commitments you are making are being made for life. You are making them to God, in the sight of God and to your future spouse. They cannot be changed.

At this point in the wedding service, the presiding minister will say:

Who giveth this woman to be married to this man?

Upon the asking of this question, it is traditional for the father of the bride to escort his daughter to the altar and present her to the groom. The exchange represents a change of responsibility between the father of the bride and the groom. The responsibility of supporting, teaching, providing, protecting, praying for, counseling and leading that which once belonged to the father is now in the hands of the groom. In the event the father of the bride is not present for this change of responsibility, the groom still accepts the responsibility by marrying the bride.

Now it is time for you to "verbally" make your commitment by repeating the vows the minister will give you. Again, this is only one example of wedding vows pulled from "The Star Book for Ministers" by Edward T. Hiscox. Many couples are now creating their own personal vows. There is nothing wrong with that just remember, the vows are not only to each other, but to God also.

I_____ take thee_____ to be my wedded wife/husband, to have and to hold from this day forward, for better or for worse, for richer or for poorer, in sickness and in health, to love and to cherish, till death us do part, according to God's holy ordinance; and thereto I plight thee my troth.

This is somewhat of the same statement that the minister read earlier, however, this time it is being verbally spoken by those who are making the commitment. When saying "I plight thee my troth," your troth is your faithfulness, fidelity, loyalty; it's your word of promise. These promises and commitments you have just made are now sealed with the presentation of the ring. Some ministers may go into an explanation of what the ring represents. It is the final statement made by the couple that seals the deal between the bride, the groom and God.

> With this ring, I thee wed: in the name of the Father, and of the Son, and of the Holy Ghost. Amen.

The minister will pray and immediately make this declaration; "Those whom God hath joined let no one put asunder." Jesus makes this very same statement in Matthew 19: 6 (NKJV) saying "So then, they are no longer two but one flesh. Therefore what God has joined together, let not man separate." That "man" He is speaking of includes the bride, the groom and all others. Through your mutual agreement, God joined you together and only God can separate you. Divorce is not an option.

In conclusion, the minister will present the couple to those present by saying:

> Forasmuch as_____ and _____ have consented together in holy wedlock, and have witnessed the same before God and this company, and thereto have given and pledged their troth, each to the other, and have declared the same by giving and receiving a ring [or rings], and by joining hands, I pronounce that they are husband and wife, in the name of the Father, and of the Son, and of the Holy Spirit. Amen.

That's it! It's a done deal. There is no turning back, no annulment, no separation, and certainly NO DIVORCE. It is right here that either the fairytale continues or the nightmare begins. The best thing about being in this situation is you (the couple) are in complete control of the direction you go. Should you choose the fairytale, you choose God's way of marriage and your fairytale will be your reality. This does not mean there will be no struggles or disappointments; it does mean that God is in control. As long as you allow Him to govern the way you relate to one another, you can overcome any obstacle presented to you. Should you face a difficult situation and not know how to escape it, KNOW THIS, God will never lead you to divorce, because it is not an option.

Author disclosure statement:

Being divorced once, I know firsthand how destructive and divisive it can be to individuals and to families. My earnest desire is that you only experience God's best in your marriage. Some might say it is hypocritical for a divorced person to boldly proclaim "divorce is not an option." Had my situation been completely and wholly my decision to make, I would not have chosen divorce. However, I did not have the understanding of marriage, nor the preparation for marriage. Therefore, my lack of knowledge and understanding led me to make some very poor decisions that eventually broke down the unity of my first marriage.

In the midst of experiencing the pain of divorce, God Himself began to teach me His way. I became so interested with this new information that my spirit craved for more and more. It seemed that in every waking moment of my life, I found myself reading, researching and seeking a deeper understanding. Then God transformed my way of thinking; He gave me a heart that matches His heart. Before long, I too began to proclaim what God proclaimed. He hates divorce.

Now it has become my mission in life to educate, counsel and encourage others in the area of marriage and divorce. My prayer is that you will use the information in this book to help prepare you for marriage and determine before saying "I do," that divorce is not an option.

CHAPTER TEN

I'm Married! Now What?

Romans 12: 16-18 NKJV "Be of the same mind toward one another. Do not set your mind on high things, but associate with the humble. Do not be wise in your own opinion. Repay no one evil for evil. Have regard for good things in the sight of all men. If it is possible, as much as depends on you, live peaceably with all men."

Husband: "We had a great time on our honeymoon! We cruised to the Bahamas, Saint Croix, and the Virgin Islands; man it was great! We made love every single day, sometimes three or four times! I couldn't tell if we were rocking the boat or if it was the waves! Man I love that girl; can't wait to spend the rest of my life with her."

Wife: "Cruise was nice. Candlelight dinners... I wore my tight fitting black dress with the back out and the girls showing, he couldn't keep his eyes or his hands off of me. All he kept saying was how much he loved me and how we would spend the rest of our lives together. We had a ball! He was so attentive, opening doors, buying me things. He is the perfect gentleman."

A few months into the marriage...

Husband: "The sex is still good, just not as often. Sometimes I wonder if she is even there. She's starting to complain about every little thing. I buy her whatever she wants, it just seems like I can't satisfy her. I keep the grass cut, take out the trash... man I swear, after we got married, she changed. She's still my girl and everything; she's the best thing that ever happened to me."

Wife: "All he seems to want is sex. I give it to him, but sometimes it's just too much. He thinks that buying me things is gonna make me happy. While I appreciate it, I need more than that. He doesn't look at me the way he used to and he never listens to me. He's still a gentleman and I'm still glad I married him but..."

These scenarios are so very typical of newlyweds. Everything starts out wonderful, like a fairytale. Through the meeting, the dating and the engagement, life together is good. Most couples get home from the honeymoon only to find themselves staring into a mirror making this statement, "I'm married, now what?" They have the skills necessary to fall in love and to get married, yet they lack understanding of how to stay in love. They lack the skills to maintain the love, romance, fun and enjoyment of being married. This becomes a point of entry for the enemy to begin his work of stealing, killing and destroying the life of a newlywed couple. So how do we live happily ever after the honeymoon phase? The answer is quite simple: the degree of difficulty in applying the answer rests squarely on your shoulders. We will get into the answer to that question in a few. First, let's look at the continuation of the previous scenario, typical of a newly married couple after a few years. Pay close attention to the subtle mental attacks of the enemy.

Scenario Three...

Husband: "SEX! What is that? Man we haven't done it since before the baby was born. She's always tired, sleepy or not in the mood. She never fixes herself up anymore; every night it's the same ole night gown, same ole rag wrapped around her head. When we talk, it's all about the baby, what he needs, what he did last night. When I said something to her about fixing herself up, she snapped at me and said, "Why don't you buy me something new? You know I can't wear that old lingerie they gave me at the bridal shower." Man, I don't know what to do. She knows the money is tight since the baby was born.'

Wife: "ALL HE THINKS ABOUT IS SEX, instead of helping me around the house and doing the things I ask him to. He doesn't realize I have two jobs: I work, then come home, take care of the baby, cook, clean and not to mention pick up behind him. I feel like I got two children. What about me? I never get any me time. When I ask him to help me out around the house, he complains about being on his feet all day and wanting to sit down for a few minutes and un-wind. Somehow his un-winding turns into him snoring like a bunch of wild hogs. Lord what have I gotten myself into?"

Believe it or not, this is so very typical of a newly married couple. There is so much truth and validity in both of these statements. What he is saying is truthful and is a logical expectation for him to have of his wife. Yet everything she is saying is also truthful and a logical expectation of her husband. So who is right and who is wrong? The answer is they are both right and they are both wrong. If you noticed, there is a very subtle hint of pride and selfishness on behalf of both parties.

The next few paragraphs will give you tips on how to live happily ever after. While you are in the preparation stage of marrying your soul mate, it is so important that you find a person who is already living according to the Word of God. If your potential mate is not living a life that is governed by God's Word, then the statements later in this chapter will be very difficult for her/him. That's worth repeating. Before you marry, make certain that the person you are considering is already living a lifestyle that reflects the Word of God.

In the first and second scenarios, life IS good. Making love multiple times a day is possible. The reality of life is that will soon change. If you are truly in love with one another, you will find simply spending time together and doing for each other, equally as rewarding and enjoyable as sex. During the meeting, dating and honeymoon stage, people tend to put on their best for the other person. People are friendly, more generous and everything seems to be fun and funny. It's only natural for a person to be on their best behavior when trying to impress someone. Who would do the opposite?

In scenario 3, we see valid complaints coming from both the husband and wife. This again is so very typical of a married couple. However, it does not have to be the case in your marriage. When both parties are actively engaged in the household affairs and they are working together to achieve a common goal, then you will create harmony.

At the core of each person's complaint you will find both pride and selfishness. These two are marriage killers; they have no place in your relationship. Both parties must compromise, but one person has to break the cycle that is destined for destruction. His complaint, like most men, is not enough sex or personal attention. The sex and romance that once existed is no longer present. He feels that his wife has turned into an "old housewife." Although he hears her complaint, his own desires (selfishness) are preventing him from "really" hearing her. Her complaints are also valid, but the complaints have an element of selfishness as well. She wants him to do more around the house and to help her with the baby. The problem is, his needs are not being met and he feels that he needs a break once he comes into the home. As long as both parties are thinking and acting this way, they are creating that cycle of destruction. You can guarantee that a situation similar to this will attempt to attack your marriage. Here is how you attack back: as the husband, recognize and appreciate all that it takes for your wife to be a mother and a wife. Decrease your expectations and increase your participation. Be sensitive to the desires and needs of both your wife and your child. Remember, women by nature are nurturers and her focus is going to be on the children often. As the man of the house, your responsibility will be to lessen the load of your wife. Sometimes it is just not practical to take a break as soon as you get home. In these cases, identify (without being told) what needs to be done around the house, then do it. Expressing your love for her by taking the pressure off of her will free her to express love towards you in the way that you desire. As a husband, you certainly have the right to sex, and your desire to see your wife looking sexy is a valid expectation. You must give consideration to how she now feels about herself sexually. Your consistent helping around the house and authentic affirmation of her beauty will cause her to respond to you in the way you desire. Get engaged with the children so that it's not always her telling you stories about the baby, but you as well. Do these things and you will slowly see the head rag come off and the sexy return.

As a wife, you must recognize just how important sex is to your husband and to the marriage. Not just "giving it to him," but actually desiring him sexually. Treating sex as a duty or responsibility will soon cause him to shy away from expressing that desire to you. This opens the door and invites the enemy in to tempt him with pornography, masturbation and even adultery. Realize that men are visual; he wants to see you sexy. Although Victoria's Secret and Frederick's are good, you can dress sexy and please him by fixing your hair, putting on a short, tight fitting t-shirt and sitting in his lap. Verbally expressing your desire for him sexually, in other words flirting, is what he desires from you most. You can't put on an outfit that will turn him on more than your verbal flirtatious expressions of desire for him. Come together with him and discuss his "winding down" time; agree on if, when, and how long this time will be.

Your husband needs you fully engaged in his life as well as you need him in yours. Understand the financial status of your home; be an active part of financial planning, saving and spending. Do not place un-necessary stress on him by asking him to spend above your means. It's the nature of a man to "come through" or "make things happen" for his family. If he is not able to do so, you should still affirm him as a man and as "your man" and your hero. If you are constantly placing unrealistic expectations on your husband, you will eventually eat away at his manhood. This can be damaging to his self-esteem and begin to create insecurities and inadequacies. It can become the door of opportunity that Satan is waiting for to introduce him to pornography and sexual immorality.

Both the husband and wife are servants of one another and must submit to one another in reverence to God. This means there are going to be times that you will find yourself doing things like picking up after him, or getting out of bed to get her a glass of water. How you respond to being a servant to your spouse will set the tone for living happily ever after.

So how do we live happily ever after?

Sit down together often and just talk. Get away, even if it's for one night; escape from day to day life. Allow yourself to become vulnerable, open up and talk about your innermost feelings, talk about your dreams, your hopes and desires. Become completely naked and unashamed before your spouse. As the listening spouse, really listen! Be prepared to ask questions to seek a deeper and better understanding of your mate. Take notes on what you can do to make life better for her/him. These are the times that will establish true intimacy. The greater the non-physical intimacy, the greater the physical intimacy will become. Most men have this backwards. They think the better sex they can give, the more their wives will see how much they love them.

Men are not from Mars, nor women from Venus! Men are from Eden and so are women. Not only are we from the same place, man and woman were made at the very same time according to Genesis 1:27. Since we were made in His image and His likeness, we have some of the same characteristics. We all have the desire to love and to be loved by someone; God loves us and desires love from us. We all desire fellowship, or friendship, people to talk and share with. We all want to know that we matter to someone else, and that someone thinks about us and cares that we exist. These are all basic needs that both men and women share. There are some differences that make us unique to our gender. Understanding our differences and catering to those differences are key to living happily ever after.

As a husband...

Understand the nature of a woman and learn to appreciate the value she brings to your life as her husband. Learn to embrace the beauty within her and the love she offers to you and your children. Women by design are nurturers, they are homemakers, they are master communicators, and they are lovers, faithful friends and confidants. Many times you don't get the best out of your wife because you fail to give her your best. As a husband, you must create an environment for her to flourish in. That environment does not include your demands and self-proclaimed title of "man of the house." The title "man of the house" must be earned and given to you by your wife. This is done by simply meeting her basic needs and adhering to the Word of God.

As a potential husband, learn these five words; be able to put them on your resume before you propose to a woman. When you commit to her, this is what you have proven you can do, and what you will do for her. These are the basic needs of a wife: Provision, Protection, Primary, Leadership and Affection. So what do they all mean?

Provision – a woman thrives in an environment where she knows that her home, her children and her lifestyle is stable. She rises to a new level when she does not have to worry about paying the bills, feeding the kids or just enjoying everyday life. As a husband, you must own the responsibility of providing for your family even if she is the majority bread-winner in the house. The responsibility of maintaining a stable lifestyle rests on you.

Protection – your wife wants to know that you are going to put her safety and the protection of the family high on your list. She wants to know that you are not going to allow her to be put in harm's way. That means she drives the best car, and you will keep her car well-maintained. She wants to know that you will not move her and the family into an un-safe neighborhood, or when things go wrong at night, you will be the first to get up. Not only are you responsible for her physical protection, but for her emotional well-being. Be in tune with what is going on with her. Protect her against the pressures of life, motherhood and her career. Don't just ask "how are you doing," but know how she's doing.

Primary – your wife wants to know that she is first in your life. Next to your relationship with God, she is most important. Make her your first choice above the softball team, above golf, Monday Night Football, or hanging out with your boys - first in everything. She wants to know that she is a very important part of your life, and that she can interrupt your day at any time for any reason.

Leadership – Contrary to popular belief, women want a man that can provide leadership for her and the family. Women are strong and very capable of setting a course for their lives, yet they desire a husband that will lead them in all aspects of life especially in their spiritual life. She wants a man who is willing to pray with her and provide spiritual guidance for her and the children.

Affection - Nothing turns your wife on more than non-sexual affection: a genuine and gentle touch or affectionate kiss that says I love you, I care about you, I think about you all day. This excites your wife and turns her on. Be willing to cross the line of wife/husband responsibility. Do the dishes, cook, clean, take care of the kids, and when you're done with that, rub her shoulders and feet while you tell her how much you love her. These are the things that a wife desires and it will keep the fire in your marriage going for a long time.

As a wife...

Understand the nature of a man and learn to appreciate the value he brings to your life as your husband. Men are simple yet widely misunderstood. Just as a woman does, men have basic needs and desires that must be met in order for him to thrive as a husband. Women tend to dismiss a man's needs be-cause he's not as vocal about it as she might be. As a wife, this may be your most difficult task; getting him to talk. Believe it or not, he is speaking however, one or two things are happening. One, you are talking so much that you can't hear him, or two, you don't understand his language. This is not a negative statement against women, as I said, women are master communicators. You must become quiet within yourself, halt the conversations you are having in your mind and allow him and his actions to speak to you. It is best to communicate with men through their basic needs which are Honor, Respect, Praise and Sex.

Honor – as a wife you honor your husband by maintaining his name and creditability among friends, relatives, business and church associates and the general community. What you do and how do you it has an impact on him. As his wife you must be trustworthy and seek to bring good and not harm to him or his reputation. A wife who honors her husband is one who is not lazy but diligent in all of her doings. She honors him by never publicly humiliating him or embarrassing him. She addresses issues privately and respectfully.

Respect – Here is one of those words that most women do not like to hear, nevertheless, it is of extreme importance to a man. It goes along with Honor. This word "respect" refers to giving regard and consideration to things said, or decisions made. Not that your opinion never matters, but there are times you must give respect to a decision that is made without having the last word or fighting to get your opinion heard. Even if you know the decision is not a good one, you sometimes have to allow him to fail. Failure builds his character. Respect his decision and pray for a favorable outcome. In the event his decision may damage the home or have a negative impact on the family, make the suggestion to seek the counsel of a neutral party that you both respect. Never disrespect him by going against a decision he has made.

Praise – Wives, you hold the ability of making or breaking your husband with the words from your mouth. You can sit him on top of the world and cause him to do mighty things. You can raise his self-worth and self-esteem by simply praising him and showing appreciation for the things he does. In fact, find three men, tell them something you admire and appreciate about them and watch them smile. You can get a man to do almost anything by praising his works and not always demanding something.

Sex – This one probably goes without saying. It is a great need and desire of a man. As his wife, you are the only person he is authorized to sexually express himself with, and it's your job to keep it that way. Sex is a connection point between the husband and wife. A man wants to feel desired sexually and to know that he is sexually satisfying to his wife. As his wife, you need to initiate sex often and make yourself sexy. Being sexy does not mean dressing up in sexy nightgowns and high-heel shoes, although that does help! A man sees you as sexy when you reflect confidence in who you are and in your ability to satisfy him. It doesn't really matter what you are wearing or how you look in sexy lingerie, or how much you weigh. What matters is your confident expression of your desire and ability to please him. This does not excuse you from presenting yourself to him in a clean, healthy and neat way.

Everything must change

If you want to live happily ever after in your marriage, understand this, things are going to change. Like George Benson sings, nothing and no one stays the same. There are many situations that can and will affect the flow of love and affection in your marriage. These things can be season changers, changing the way you relate to one another, such as the birth of a child, the death of a loved one, loss of employment, infidelity, relocation, empty nest and the list goes on. The thing that should remain consistent and will keep the love alive is your commitment to "agape." That is a commitment to love one another unconditionally. Through it all and at the end of it all, love, true love, agape love will prevail.

Recognize when there is a season change in your relationship, then make necessary adjustments to keep the love and romance alive. Life happens, yet it keeps going. You will be disappointed by your mate at some point; likewise, you will be disappointing to your mate. Through ups and can't-get-ups, agape stands firm in its position to express the absolute best that love can offer.

CHAPTER ELEVEN

Quick Tips for Living Happily Ever After

Tip #1 Pray together

Praying is a method of communicating with God the Father. He is just that, "the Father." He desires to hear from you, to meet your needs, to provide for you and to protect you. When you come before God as a couple, He sees you as He did Adam and Eve, naked and not ashamed. He desires you in your most pure and vulnerable form. It is right here that God hears your heart and your marriage will be strengthened daily. Pray for each other. You should know the desires of your spouse; know what she/he is believing God for. Intercede on their behalf by asking God to fulfill their desires. Pray for their health, physical and emotional well-being.

Tip #2 Serve one another in love

When you fall in love with Jesus, your desires become all about pleasing Him. In doing so, your desires are met by Him. The same applies to your marriage. When you serve one another out of reverence to God, He honors you and your marriage. The cycle of love begins here and it never ends, it only grows continually.

Tip #3 Date each other regularly

Dating does not mean just going to dinner and movies together, it means be in HOT pursuit of your spouse the way you did before you were married. Get dressed up, get a haircut, put on those jeans she loves to see you in, shave and wear her favorite cologne. Ladies, when you get dressed for work, you do that for you. When you are dating your husband, you get dressed for him. The entire date is about your spouse. Sexual fulfillment is not the goal; it is connecting with your spouse and expressing your delight of just being together.

Tip #4 Be best friends

Life and marriage are about the relationship. If there is any one person that you should be able to talk with and be completely vulnerable, it's your spouse. Set it in your heart to be a better friend to your spouse than they are to you. Others will attempt to assume that position in your life; you must recognize it and re-direct it quickly. Bring all of your hurts, disappointments, fears, desires and so on, to your best friend, your spouse. Allow Jesus to be the primary example of what a true friend really is.

Tip #5 Talk often

One of the top reasons given for divorce is a lack of communication. Your entire relationship is built on how you communicate and respond to one another. Commit to making time to sit down and dive into the world of your spouse. KNOW what is going on with them; be in tune to their feelings. Daydream together; take walks or bike rides together. Open your mouth and allow what is going on in your heart to come out. If you are the listener, really listen; repeat and re-state to ensure understanding. Follow-up with them later to see how the situation is going and become fully engaged in their world.

The best way to break down a unit or team is to destroy their ability to communicate. You see it in wars and even at football games; if the crowd can make enough noise that the team cannot hear the quarterback, the play is disrupted. Satan's desire is to make enough noise between you and your spouse so that you cannot hear each other or the voice of God. Make it a point to ACTIVELY communicate with your spouse daily.

Tip #6 Mentors

We learn a lot by reading however, our learning is more effective and memorable when we can witness someone else actually doing it. Find a couple that has the type of marriage that you desire. This should be a couple with a proven track record of wisdom and has many years of experience at being married. This couple can help you see past today's issues and into the future. They should be people whom you know and respect and whose judgment you value. They will be able to help you resolve disagreements and close the door on arguments and miscommunications.

Tip #7 Commit to working through your problems

In your anger, do not sin. Do not let the sun go down while you are still angry, and do not give the devil a foothold (Ephesians 4:26-27 NIV). Begin all contentious conversations with love and allow the agape love that is commanded by God, to guide your words and responses. You may not be able to resolve an issue overnight, but agree to park the issue and re-address it as soon as possible. In this case, embrace one another as you verbally express your love and commitment to the marriage before parting for the day or going to bed at night. Use the Word of God as your guide to resolution. If you still cannot agree, then seek the help of your mentors.

Tip #8 Live the Word

Allow the Word to govern your way of thinking and living. God knows best how a marriage is to work and His Word is our guide to living a peaceful, productive and righteous lifestyle. Colossians 3:15-16 NKJV "And let the peace of God rule in your hearts, to which also you were called in one body; and be thankful. Let the Word of Christ dwell in you richly in all wisdom, teaching and admonishing one another in psalms and hymns and spiritual songs, singing with grace in your hearts to the Lord."

Tip #9 For husbands...

Support your wife in her ambitions and desires. Help her become all of what God has called her to be. It is in your unselfish acts of sacrifice that she begins to blossom and God will honor you and bless you for your obedience to His Word. Learn how Christ loved the church then love your wife in that same manner. Make her and the family a priority in your life; make certain that she never feels neglected or fears lack. Always re-assure her through your actions as well as your words, of your desire and ability to take care of her and the family.

Tip #10 For wives...

Be his biggest cheerleader! Your husband needs to know that you are on his side no matter what. Do not allow another person to encourage or celebrate your husband more than you.

Honor him, respect him, praise him and don't forget, love him sexually!

Tip #11 Forgiveness

We all make mistakes. We all have our own selfish little ways. Learn how to forgive and move on towards a happy and loving marriage. Remember, forgiveness is not about the other person getting away with something; it's about you getting free from the offense. Un-forgiveness places a weight around your neck and it keeps you from living and loving as God has commanded you to.

Tip #12 Live, love and learn

Life is about people and the relationship that you have with them. Learn to enjoy and take full advantage of the special people God has allowed to be in your life. Visit, talk, take walks, vacation, play games, learn how to put away the stresses of life and to embrace the meaning of life. It is not about material possessions, fame, power or financial gain, but laughing, smiling and loving your friends and family.

Tip #13 Divorce is not an option

Remove the word divorce from your marriage dictionary. Do not allow it to ever come up in your conversations or your thoughts. Don't even joke about it with your friends. God's desire is for you to have a marriage that exceeds your expectations. God is committed to giving you a glorious marriage. Join Him by committing to let Him lead you by His Word, through prayer and through the spiritual counsel He will place around you.

ABOUT THE AUTHOR

Winston Tyrone Jackson, Sr.

After a successful tour in the Marine Corps, Winston spent the next 15 years climbing the corporate ladder working for several Fortune 500 companies. With seemingly everything a man could possibly want: family, great job, being a restaurant owner, and being a church leader, one thing was missing: a true understanding of God's design of marriage. After 21 years of marriage, it all came to a halt. Marriage, house, cars, job, and business all disappeared like a vapor. "With $40 to my name, a borrowed car, no job and living with my mother at age 46, God began to rebuild me." God has given Winston wisdom, knowledge, and understanding on the subject of marriage. He has been blessed with a new life, new wife and most of all a passion for others who are struggling in their marriage. He is a mentor to several young couples, as well as single men and women desiring to be married.

In 2011, Winston published his first book entitled "Marriage – 21 years of Doing it Wrong, 21 Days to Make it Right." This powerful 21 day devotional was written using the concept of sowing seeds of love into your marriage and allowing God to produce the harvest. Winston has been a guest speaker at several churches within the Florida/Georgia area. He has appeared on Pure Radio's "Terry & Terry Show" as well as on TCT's "Athletes with Purpose Show" with former NFL Player Frank Murphy.

In November of 2013, Winston released his second book entitled "Preparing to Date Your Soul Mate." This book targets singles who desire to one day marry the person that God has for them. It's a thought provoking look into the preparation it takes to be the best possible mate that God has to offer another. The book takes you through various stages of relationship such as falling in love with Jesus, living single while waiting for your mate, and how to attract the person you really want to be with. It also provides insightful information on premarital counseling, establishing mentors, financial planning and an in-depth look and understanding of the wedding vows.

For more information about Winston, visit his website or contact him via Facebook or email:

Website: www.winstontjacksonsr.com

FB: www.facebook.com/winstontjacksonsr

Email: winstontjackson@yahoo.com

Book Order Form

"Renew your mind to God's Design"
To order copies of this book and other books by Winston Tyrone Jackson, Sr., indicate the number of copies you would like next to the title, provide your shipping address and contact information, enclose payment including shipping, and mail this form to:

Winston T. Jackson, Sr.
P.O. Box 442343
Jacksonville, Fl. 32222

- Preparing to Date Your Soul Mate @ $9.99 each _____
- Marriage: *21 Days of Doing it Wrong,*
  21 Days to Make it Right @$9.99 each _____

Shipping and Handling: $5.00

Total Enclosed: _____

Shipping Address:

Name: _____

Street: _____

City, State, Zip_____

Phone: _____

Email: _____

Notes